The Bible for Every Day

ISAAC AND JACOB

ISAAC AND JACOB

Genesis 24-36

Ronald S. Wallace

Thomas Nelson Publishers
Nashville • Camden • New York

To
the study group at
College Park Presbyterian Church

Contents

CONTENTS

CONTENTS

CONTENTS

Introduction

Throughout my earlier parish ministry I had many interested lay people, some receptive, some critical (I do not know to which I am most indebted) who came to church services to hear the Word of God interpreted in its relevance especially to our personal lives, but also to the Church and the world. They believed, as I did, that Christ himself comes into the midst to enable us to understand the Scriptures within the fellowship of his people, as he did on the road to Emmaus, and they expected to hear his voice. They were willing to gather in small groups to discuss passages with me and with one another.

When I later became a theological teacher, I was able to devote much more time to the study of the current and traditional exegetical and critical discussion amongst scholars, and I became better informed on background and historical matters. But when I tried to convey all this to my students in an academic way, I was unhappy. Some of them knew the languages better than I could remember, and in any case, with little trouble most of them could find everything I was trying to convey to them in other people's commentaries.

I decided, therefore, to return to what I had previously been used to doing, and knew better—and to try to do it more expertly now, and as much as possible to the standard of scholarship expected within an academic environment.

For the warm response of the students I shall always be grateful. They came now in comparatively large numbers, with their wives, and other lay people and pastors—and with the same kind of desire to hear and willingness to listen as I had previously found in a congregation.

The books in this series are the product of this continuing ministry. But instead of taking the form of textual sermons or a series of lectures, they have been arranged to take the reader continuously through the printed biblical text, sometimes from chapter to chapter, sometimes from oracle to oracle, sometimes from incident to incident and sometimes from verse to verse, following the order of the text, and trying not to leave out what is important or what might be difficult. They are arranged in easily readable units divided by carefully chosen headings. This arrangement will enable those who customarily have a daily Bible reading to use the book for such a purpose.

These books in no way seek to replace the standard academic commentary to which I myself owe many important insights. But they are the product of a slightly different approach to the text. This approach, arising as it does out of different presuppositions from those of many academic commentators, sometimes forces one to come to different conclusions from theirs about the origin and integrity of the text, and the intention of the original author.

I have often been encouraged by pastors who have found my books or lectures helpful in preparing their sermons. These studies are written with a personal understanding of this need for help in pulpit work.

RONALD S. WALLACE

ISAAC AND JACOB

Genesis 24-36

1

On Marriage and Family Life

GENESIS 24.1-9, 62-7

From altar to hearth

The book of Genesis is about the birth of a nation as well as about the birth of the world. God begins to create a people for himself and for his purposes. Chosen specially by him, nurtured and trained by him with infinite care, blessed by him, they are destined to bring to the world's history, and into all human affairs, fresh vitality, a revolutionary outlook and direction. Through this 'people of God', indeed, 'salvation' is to be brought to all mankind. Its founders are to be Abraham, Isaac and Jacob.

Our first picture of Abraham came when God called him to go from Haran to Canaan.

> Go from your country . . . to the land that I will show you. And I will make of you a great nation, and I will bless you, and make your name great, so that you will be a blessing . . . and by you all the families of the earth shall bless themselves (Gen. 12.1-3).

Now we see him *old, well-advanced in years* (v. 1), approaching his deathbed. He has only one more task to accomplish, one final important decision to make.

He has nobody beside him at this time and he is praying to God. Solitude has been an outstanding characteristic of his life. It is true he often depended on his wife Sarah, and sometimes they had to find out God's will together. But more often he has been forced to decide alone, often at one of the altars he built—before God only, and in the impenetrable depth of the human heart. These chapters about him

3

could have been called with justice *The Book of the Lonely Pilgrim.*

The rest of this long transitional chapter and the stories about Abraham's successors, however, immerse us deeper into the intimate and mundane details of home life. Both Isaac and Jacob, whose careers we now follow, are depicted as family men. Certainly, on occasion, both have personal encounters with God, and in Jacob's case especially these moments are dramatic and memorable. But even in these solitary encounters of Jacob with God it is the pressure of family affairs that has driven him into the solitude, and his mind never ceases to be full of his family's problems. Indeed, the new section of the book of Genesis which now takes up the continuous story of both these men could be called *The Book of Family Life.*

The hearth, as well as the altar, is now seen as the place of destiny. Occasional family celebrations and family tensions which we have read about in the Abraham stories have now become the order of the day. The destiny of the people of God, which in the earlier chapters has been seen to depend almost entirely on sublime and dramatic interventions—on God talking from above to the lone soul—is now seen to be brought about no less effectively through the way his people act, react and interact in their lives together at home, through their approach to marriage and the children they have, and through the way they go about their family affairs.

A marriage made in heaven

The beginning of family life is shown as all-important. Isaac is 'getting on in years' and still unwed. He desperately needs companionship: his mother has just died. Born late in his parents' lives, he has had an unusual and restricted upbringing. Hardly a woman in the world would have been able to understand him. But, far away as distance was then reckoned, there is one woman as unique as Isaac himself. She has been brought up in the only place in the outside world where the deep-seated beliefs that have kept this boy apart from others and so close to his father and mother can find understanding and sympathy. In her family tradition there has been the same talk of God, the same kind of piety and the memory of a promise that embraced all nations. She knows that Terah, the founder of her family, and Abraham her uncle were inspired by it, each in his day. God has been at work here as well as in Canaan, preparing and keeping this woman and this man for each other.

The responsibility for arranging family marriages belonged to the parent. Abraham believes he must find for Isaac a woman who will share the same faith as he has in the same God. Without such a basis no marriage can work. Such a woman is probably living in his old homestead where his own roots used to be. He will send his servant to look for her. He feels sure that if God has been at work preparing her she will be *willing* to come (vv. 5, 8).

Marvellously Rebekah is ready. She is in no way bought from her guardian or compelled by him: 'We will call the maiden and ask her . . . will you go . . .? She said, I will go' (vv. 57-8).

Isaac, too, takes her as freely as she gives herself to him. Their marriage takes place in an atmosphere dominated by a genuine devotion and gratitude to God on the part of both.

Isaac went out to meditate in the field in the evening; and he lifted up his eyes and looked, and behold, there were camels coming. And Rebekah . . . took her veil and covered herself. And the servant told Isaac all the things that he had done. Then Isaac brought her into the tent, and took Rebekah, and she became his wife; and he loved her (vv. 63-7).

They fall in love with each other and it seems even to be 'love at first sight'. But the basis and stability and success of the marriage depend on earlier and more primary ingredi-

5

ents—on God's work and on their shared faith in him—which are there even before the romance begins.

In his own teaching about marriage Jesus went back to these earliest chapters of the book of Genesis. Neither divorce nor polygamy was to be regarded as having any place in the way God meant human life to be lived. He called on his hearers to ignore the fact that the law of Moses had permitted such things. Men and women must no longer allow themselves to be drawn back into the multi-marital family messes that Jacob, David and Solomon fell into. With his own additions he quoted the words of Genesis 2.24:

> Have you not read that he who made them from the beginning made them male and female, and said, 'For this reason a man shall leave his father and mother and be joined to his wife, and the two shall become one flesh'? So they are no longer two but one flesh. What therefore God has joined together, let no man put asunder (Matt. 19.4-6).

His pattern was the same as that outlined in this story—one destined for another, and the two joined together in a union that God alone can create and God alone dissolve. Marriage, as with Isaac and Rebekah, involves the task of working out in the midst of all life's joys and sorrows or difficulties what has been decreed in heaven.

Questions from contrasting worlds

The pressures upon traditional customs today inevitably make us question the presuppositions we have brought out from the story. In our present society the home is often no longer regarded as the basic, stable unit of society. Once, when home influence meant something good, the word 'father' could be used for God, but today 'father' can seem a rather questionable name for the deity. Nor is the home seen as unequivocally good—do we not sometimes even recommend the break-up of home life on the ground that the alternative of sticking together is much worse? In the cities of the USA, where guns are easily and cheaply bought, a large proportion of the murders that are thus made possible are committed within the intimate home circle.

Community life being as it is today, how can we still believe that God is working his great purposes out gradually, quietly and surely through our marriages; through the quarrelling, the suppression, the isolation, the bitterness, the violence—the domestic prison? Our thoughts for social and individual reform turn, rather, towards the ballot-box, the lobbies of parliament, the protest marches, and perhaps even to terrorism—and we think about the possibility that the finger will come down on the push-button and start a nuclear war.

Many people today have doubts about the old idea that one man was intended for one woman and that sex is meant to be only in the second place, and after marriage. Does the way it begins and who it begins with really matter so much? Should it not be made easily possible that if a mistake is made at the start we can break off and begin again? Therefore we experiment. We cease to think about marriages being made by God; and we justify cheaply obtained divorce. In today's atmosphere would not even Isaac and Rebekah have broken their marriage up when their children were teenagers and their problems and misunderstandings were at their worst?

A plea of relevance

Many aspects of the Bible's teaching are relevant in answer to such questions. Its stories about family life are stories about exactly our kind of modern family life—full of tragic failures, bitter disappointments, even betrayals, and always in tension. Here in the book of Genesis we have husband against wife, wife against husband, in-law against in-law,

7

brother against brother. In the case of Esau and Jacob the situation becomes so bad that the dear favourite has to leave home—for good. It is as if God is saying to us: 'I know all about it, and I am in it in spite of it all!'

Christ comes to enable us to make a new beginning with everything on earth. This means that however bad a start has been made, nothing is irretrievable with God. In matters of marriage and sex many people today become involved in the most enslaving and miserable mix-up that life and the devil can produce. It is precisely here that Christ wants to come and work with his power to sort things out and to cancel not only the guilt but even, often, the justifiable human consequences of the past. If the power of the gospel cannot enable new creative beginnings to take place within this particular sphere, then it is inadequate for human life. In Cana of Galilee (John 2.1–11) Jesus at a critical point, when the celebration was threatened, turned water into wine and enabled the party to continue. It was a sign that he had come from God into human life to work creatively and powerfully in this same way whenever the joy and vitality of anything good are beginning to collapse—especially so where marriage and home are concerned. The people around him had only to invite him in, to ask his help and obey his word.

Jesus again and again gave signs that he was concerned not only with marriage but with every aspect of the home. Distracted parents brought their children to him. He mended the severed relationships. He restored son to mother (Luke 7.15), son to father (Mark 9.17 ff.), daughter to mother (Matt. 15.22 ff.), daughter to father (Matt. 9.18 ff.), brother to sister (John 11.38 ff.). His last miracle of all took place in the midst of a family gathering (John 11.17 ff.), as had his first at Cana (John 2.1 ff.).

The Bible never fails to stress the fact that God wills to work out his purposes in the world through family life as well as within it. Of course the political front is always given its due importance. As a developing people, Israel was to discover that what happened in the upper councils of their national life could either further or thwart God's purposes for their nation, and God raised up prophets to tell them so. They discovered too that a tyrant from a great empire could come sweeping down through their countryside to cause devastation. They too had to take to the battlefield with their leaders or kings to fight things out for weal or woe.

But while all this is recognized, persistently the responsibility for the destiny of the nation was laid on the parents to live and pass on the faith, and on the children to receive and live the faith. If we fail here we fail in God's purposes. The tragedy of David's later life is told simply as a long illustration of how the destiny of each individual, and the destiny of the nation too, depend on how home life is lived.

In the New Testament the emphasis is on the Church, but the Church grows and continues to grow as in each generation men and women, like Abraham, hear themselves called, and as Christian marriages are made, and homes appear, at the centre of its growing life.

A radio programme once broadcast a play about a strike in a factory. During the strike there happened to be difficulties at home for two of those chiefly responsible. One of the directors was having trouble with his adolescent children. The most influential shop steward was quarrelling bitterly with his wife. The talks for a settlement went badly. But somehow, marvellously, the director's teenagers began to take their father's advice. And the steward and his wife made it up. These troubles had no direct connection with the factory business. Yet immediately there the atmosphere at the negotiating table changed, and a solution was found. The plot in this particular instance may seem too neat to be true to life, but the dramatist had a message for our times. We evade facing up to our home life and working out the issues on this front only at our peril. Flight from family responsibility is flight from what is meant to bring us to our own true destiny, and it may also be flight from our

9

responsibility for the world, and for the true social well-being of the people around us.

2

The Searching and the Finding

GENESIS 24.10-61

'The Lord . . led me'

God *'guided my steps'* (v. 27 JB). He guided the searching and the finding. Each step of the way was perfectly planned by him. The preparations for the journey have proved adequate, the gifts are exactly those required to impress the covetous brother Laban. The meetings, the conversations, and their outcome, all seem to be exactly controlled by providence. The mind of each person concerned is oriented by God. Their thoughts harmonize and they share the same sense of urgency. All resistance to the final purpose is removed. A silent and secret prayer is inspired and answered almost at the moment it is uttered.

All this is extraordinary even for the Bible's account of life. Only occasionally does the Bible give us such a vivid picture of the detailed and exact guidance of God. We have Saul's journey in search of his father's asses with the extraordinary coincidences which enabled him to find Samuel and to hear the important message the prophet was waiting to give him (1 Sam. 9). There are similar stories in the New Testament. After a long frustrating period in Asia, Paul saw a vision telling him to go over to Macedonia. Immediately he found the winds and the weather favourable

10

and was soon guided exactly to the place where he met Lydia, whose heart 'the Lord opened' (Acts 16.1 ff.).

Of course we should not require the evidence of such marvellous coincidences. It is basic to our faith to believe that God has control of each step of our way. But often events are so strangely in contradiction to what we hoped for from him that we find it difficult to believe we are in his hands. 'Thy way was through the sea, thy path through the great waters; yet thy footprints were unseen' (Ps. 77.19), wrote the Psalmist, describing for us how we must often expect to be led. We seldom realize, at the time, how important certain encounters, certain conversations are for our whole future, though we can look back years later to see that God was there making a decision for us, perhaps even against our will, and controlling things wonderfully. How thrilled we would have been had we known *then* what was happening!

The extraordinary in the ordinary

Though everything was extraordinary on this day it is important to notice at the same time how remarkably *ordinary* it was. Often in the Bible when God is seen to guide events there is a vision, an intervention from heaven. Abraham was treated in this way: 'Then the Lord appeared . . . and said' (Gen. 12.7). Hagar was guided by an angel (Gen. 16.7 ff.), Moses by a miracle and a word (Exod. 3.1 ff.).

But in this present chapter there is no vision, no apparent intervention from above to disturb the natural course of events. There is not even a 'word' from above. God does not intrude. He simply allows ordinary things to work together with such perfect timing that the ordinary becomes extraordinary. Moreover he makes the participants conscious that he is there behind these pedestrian events, working everything out for good. It is Calvin who puts it concisely: God

11

does the extraordinary in an ordinary way, he tells us, and 'he directs the minds of his servants towards it'

Here we are close to New Testament teaching, especially to that of Jesus. Jesus always lived with a sense of being guided by his heavenly Father. Sometimes guidance came to him by dramatic intervention from above (John 12.28; Mark 9.4), but more often the plan of his life was unfolded before him through coincidences and concurrences that took place on the ordinary level. He looked out for such remarkable coincidences. For example, when he met the woman at the well he recognized that God had brought her to him at that moment—he sensed her critical situation, read her secret thoughts and spoke the words he felt the situation inspired. He saw too that her salvation could become the key to the salvation of her whole community (John 4).

Jesus sought to make us, too, sensitive to what God might be seeking to do to us and through us in the ordinary course of our daily life as we seek to give ourselves to his service. Abraham taught his servant to think of life as if an angel were there to go before him, beckoning and guiding (Gen. 24.7). Jesus deliberately put himself in the place of the angel in the story. He described himself as the Good Shepherd who puts out his sheep and goes before them to lead them, especially by letting them 'hear his voice' (John 10.1 ff.). This can mean the gentle inner voice—the familiar voice—which often comes to us quite quietly as we read and think about the Scriptures or hear them preached, and at the same time look around us. We should try to become more sensitive to the possibility of the extraordinary happening even to us on the ordinary levels of life.

Of course Abraham's steward also claims to have led himself! He discussed his course with Abraham beforehand and chose what he thought was the best way. He then set out in it so that God might guide him. The Authorized Version brings out the point perfectly in its translation of verse 27: *I being in the way, the Lord led me to the home of my master's brethren.*

We sometimes have to find the door into God's presence and guidance simply by first setting out on the way, perhaps by meditating about what the Bible is saying to us, backed up by an initial act of obedience.

The prayer

The servant's prayer started off the extraordinary chain of events:

> *O Lord, God of my master Abraham, grant me success today . . . Behold, I am standing by the spring of water . . . Let the maiden to whom I shall say, 'Pray let down your jar that I may drink', and who shall say, 'Drink, and I will water your camels'—let her be the one whom thou hast appointed for thy servant Isaac By this I shall know that thou hast shown steadfast love to my master* (vv. 12-14).

Much of the prayer is in traditional phraseology which he would have learnt from Abraham. But the words 'grant me success', a modern commentator points out, are profane and 'do not belong to religious vocabulary'. The essential thing in prayer is for us to 'let our request be made known to God' (cf. Phil. 4.6). We can often do this effectively if we use the words that come to us naturally. This man put himself into his prayer.

The sheer boldness and *naïveté* of the request must raise questions in our minds. It is easy to criticize and warn others against imitating it. What right have we, in prayer, to outline as this man did the exact way we expect God to work in answer? Prayer should be wiser and more subdued! But God does not expect a sophisticated approach from those who are newly experiencing their faith—there is time for that to develop. Moreover he is not praying for himself. He is serving another in an extraordinarily difficult situation, and

Abraham his master whom he trusts absolutely has pledged that God will 'prosper him in his mission' (Gen. 24.7).

In a more mature approach to prayer we should ask for what God has already promised to us in his word—turning his promises into prayers—and we should take the requests of the Lord's Prayer as our chief model. We can be confident in our praying if God has already encouraged us to pray in this way. But even cautious and wise Calvin says that this general rule 'does not prevent the Lord, when he determines to give something extraordinary, from directing the minds of his servants towards it; not that he would lead them away from his word, but only that he makes some peculiar concession to them in their mode of praying.'

Luther suggests, however, that the servant is merely expressing a wish. The man, he believed, was completely perplexed and was uttering a sigh: 'O that the virgin who is to be the bride of the son of my Lord would come!' And he urges us to take courage from the fact that *before he had done speaking, behold, Rebekah . . . came out with her water jar* (v. 45). He quotes Isaiah: 'Before they call, I will answer, while they are yet speaking, I will hear' (Isa. 65.24). He could have added the verse from Psalm 138: 'On the day I called thou didst answer me' (Ps. 138.3).

The Bible is always realistic about our obtaining answers to our prayers. It acknowledges that often they are long in coming, and sometimes they seem never to come. It refuses simple explanations. But it points out that sometimes prayers *are* dramatically and quickly answered. No doubt it is because we are sometimes given such answers that we find the courage to continue to pray for other things without any immediate answer. 'Brethren, do not despise your prayers,' says Luther again (this time quoting Bernard), 'but know that as soon as you begin to pray, your prayer is read, and written down at once in the presence of Divine Majesty.'

The sense of the presence of God

The Old Testament often shows us people suddenly gripped by the conviction that God has broken abruptly the ordinary routine of their lives and is there before them saying something of infinite significance. On one occasion Abraham was seized with this sense of God's infinite nearness. Three visitors arrived at his door, and before receiving them into his house he suddenly realized that God was there, coming to sit at his table! Moses experienced the same realization at the burning bush. Sometimes God seemed to clothe his presence in an object or a vision or sometimes in a miracle.

Abraham's servant is without such signs that God was there, yet he sensed his presence. He suddenly sees that God is not simply controlling him from a distance, but is actually close at hand in a unique way within the very events of that day. The New English Bible rightly translates verse 26: *So the man bowed down and prostrated himself to the Lord.*

Everything that happens around him is now miraculous; God is within it. Rebekah comes with him so willingly; an obstinate guardian like Laban releases her—it is as if they too sense the same presence.

Usually in the Bible when people know themselves confronted by God they are filled with awe and fall on their faces (Isa. 6.5; Acts 22.7). Nearly always this experience is accompanied by a sense of urgency. They want to know exactly what God wants and they hurry to begin to do it (Isa. 6.8; Acts 22.10). This servant is no exception. *Do not delay me*, he says when they try to make him tarry a week or two in Paddan-aram with his mission half accomplished. *Since the Lord has prospered my way; let me go* (vv. 56 ff.). God, he feels, has given events a momentum that must not be held back. To try to delay the fulfilment of what God has begun so powerfully and gloriously would be sacrilege. Rebekah herself seems to share his anxiety to seize the

15

impulse of the moment and not to quench the Spirit by procrastination.

Jesus moved on even as he called people to follow him. There can be no delay. If we want him to be with us and we with him, we have to go to be where he is: we cannot try to draw him back to where we want to remain (cf. John 12.26).

> He who does not rise for the Holy Spirit in the very hour or at the very moment he calls will never take hold of him [says Luther] for the Holy Spirit does not return when He has once gone away . . . I have learned from my own experience that whenever it was necessary to pray, to read, or partake of the Lord's Supper, the longer I delayed the more disinclined I was.

He quotes Bonaventure: 'He who abandons opportunity will be abandoned by opportunity.' It is vitally important in the service of God to see a thing through, faithfully and promptly, to the end, once we have been inspired to begin.

The master in the servant

Before Abraham dies, we are shown a faint sign of the fulfilment of the promise that God made to him at the beginning: 'You will be a blessing . . . and by you all the families of the earth shall bless themselves' (Gen. 12.1). We glimpse the strength of the old man's influence—especially on his servant.

The servant seems to have caught Abraham's faith. Instinctively he seems to pray as Abraham would have prayed and to trust God as Abraham would have done. Abraham must have seen the man's faith growing over many years, for this man's vexatious behaviour in the earlier days was the occasion of a complaint he made once to God (Gen. 15.2, cf. *Abraham*, p. 42).

Obviously, therefore, this is the result of years of patient teaching (cf. Gen. 18.19). Little by little Abraham has persevered in speaking about God, life, providence and prayer—teaching given not only by a father to a son but by the employer to his employee! Of course it is also the result of personal influence. The servant has watched Abraham for many years, seen his reaction to threats, trials, joys, disappointment, tragedy and death, and he has come to believe in the God who can make such a man out of the ordinary stuff of humanity. No other kind of god could have made a man so good to know.

Above all, what has happened to the servant is the result of Abraham's praying. The old man is weak, possibly faint in spirit too; perhaps he has had to drag himself to prayer and to toil on his bed to keep himself awake and alert to pray. But pray he does, and all the while these extraordinary things are happening in Paddan-aram, his prayers are being heard and answered.

3

From One Generation to Another

GENESIS 25.1-26

A parenthesis—the death, burial and descendants of Abraham

Abraham, having done everything that God required of him in connection with the promise, and having done it well, is not allowed to depart without mention of an episode which, we believe, belonged far back in his past life. At some point in those early days, certainly after his marriage to Sarah, he took to himself another wife called Keturah and had

17

numerous offspring by her (vv. 1-4; cf. 1 Chron. 1.32). Judged by the normal standards of his day it was an allowable thing, and Abraham himself can have made no attempt to hide it.

But as far as the modern reader is concerned, a reader who is to learn to revere Abraham as a great man of God, this lapse in particular, which did not later affect his response to God's command and promise, seems to be regarded as better left unmentioned till we have been able fully to evaluate the man's otherwise outstanding greatness. It need be given only bracketed mention at the end because it was forgiven by God. But it has to be brought up at this point, when Abraham is about to die, for we are to be assured that he died with all his affairs in order. There were six sons born to Keturah. Before he went, Abraham settled any debt he had towards them in a generous way. They prospered and had important descendants (vv. 2-6).

Possibly, too, by bringing the matter up at this point, the narrator is quietly hinting to us that in face of death it is better to bring everything into the open. Life for so many of us is uncomfortable because we have too big a burden of hidden things, and of past affairs not yet properly accounted for. But as we come nearer to death and, we hope, to God, we tend not to *want* to hide anything any more. We desire, rather, the health and liberty that a full exposure and settlement of the past can give.

A number of commentators read the story in such a way as to imply that Abraham actually married Keturah *after* Sarah died, and that he had these six children in his extreme old age. This belief caused Augustine to express his wonder at the persistent bonus of the renovated vigour given to the old man when God enabled him to beget Isaac. Luther accepted this view, approved Augustine's theory about Abraham's rejuvenation, and though he disapproved of the 'seemingly bad example that gravely offends everyone' he insisted that the old man's motive was not lasciviousness but 'eager desire to obtain offspring' in view of the promise: 'You shall be the father of many nations.' Calvin frankly calls Abraham's action foolish and unworthy and pities him in the 'decrepitude of his old age'.

The discussion is all so confusing that we hurry to quote Luther's summing up: 'Let us bury the most saintly Patriarch Abraham whose example very much deserves to be preserved for ever in the Church of God.' At the burial Ishmael was there with Isaac at the Cave of Machpelah (v. 9). We are now told that in addition to the children of Keturah Abraham's descendants by Ishmael number twelve, who were all themselves princes and founders of nations. When the narrator here underlines all these distant links in the past between Abraham and many peoples, is he expressing a hope that one day a great multitude may come to value this common link as they come to sit down with Abraham in the Kingdom of God in order to share in the blessing promised to all nations (cf. Matt. 8.11)?

The promise and the prayer

That Abraham at this time *gave all he had to Isaac* (v. 5) can mean that he acknowledged him as his first-born heir, in some solemn public statement such as was then a widespread custom, regarded as having the validity that a written and signed will would have today. Abraham believed at the same time, no doubt, that he was passing on to his successor all the unique privileges and responsibilities which God had laid on himself in giving him the promise: 'I will bless you . . . you will be a blessing . . . by you all families of the earth shall bless themselves' (Gen. 12.1ff.).

Later on in his own life, when he felt he was near death, Isaac tried to pass on both the birthright of the first-born and the blessing of the promise to his favourite son Esau in much the same way as Abraham had transmitted it all to him. We cannot doubt that being entrusted with all this

19

privilege and responsibility in such a way meant much to him, and the prosperity and happiness that came to him in the early years of his married life seemed to confirm him in his dedication: *After the death of Abraham God blessed Isaac his son* (v. 11).

Rebekah was entirely one with him in this purpose when she left her home in Paddan-aram. Knowing her strange interest in the promise that had been given to their Uncle Abraham, her own relatives had pronounced upon her, in their own belligerent way, their own form of the blessing and wish that she might share fruitfully in the fulfilment of the great promise: 'Our sister, be the mother of thousands of ten thousands; and may your descendants possess the gate of those who hate them!' (Gen. 24.60).

Therefore, of course, it was all the greater shock, and all the more bitter a trial, when the couple began to face the fact that Rebekah in the normal course of affairs might be childless: *And Isaac prayed to the Lord for his wife, because she was barren* (v. 21). The suggestion is that at this stage he did the praying on her behalf, as well as for himself. He seems at this point a little isolated. But Rebekah herself is in his prayer, and it is all the more passionate because he loves her so much, and he knows how desperate she is.

How mixed are Isaac's motives in all this praying. He is also praying for the fulfilment of God's promise for the furtherance of God's will and Kingdom. He is praying for his own domestic happiness and for his wife to have the privilege of motherhood. His prayer is heavenly and spiritual. It is also quite earthly and natural. The Lord's Prayer gives us the same mixture. Its first few clauses about the name, the Kingdom and the will of God being done are all heavenly, all about the fulfilment of the promises and orientate us away from our own personal needs. The last few clauses about our daily bread, evils and temptations are earthly, express our natural desires and deal with our need for relief from and within our miseries.

Of course our prayer life must become dominated by the 'spiritual', by seeking first the Kingdom of God and his glory and his will (Matt. 6.33). But whatever upsets us, deprives us of what we think should be our basic human rights or basic measure of human happiness, whatever makes our wives or husbands or children or dear friends miserable and frustrated or puts them in danger can legitimately find a place in our praying. Indeed we need not be ashamed if it is these things that drive us most urgently to pray. For such things belong to God and his Kingdom and are his concern.

War in the womb and dread in the mind

When the answer to Isaac's prayer comes, Rebekah should be the happiest woman in the world. Her motherly heart is satisfied, and God is now using her to fulfil his purposes. From an earthly point of view, moreover, she is fortunate. Her husband is becoming increasingly wealthy. He is a kind man, not difficult to live with, and full of concern for her happiness and comfort at this time. Now she can prepare with serene joy for the birth of her child.

But, inexplicably, the period of pregnancy proves to be more difficult for her than the previous years of frustration have been. She consults others. She finds that there is more than normal movement by the foetus in her womb, and it keeps her awake and troubles her mind. In her occasional moods of depression she speaks as if she wishes to die. *The children struggled with one another inside her, and she said, 'If this is the way of it, why go on living?'* (v. 22 JB).

Luther suggested that she supposed herself to be carrying 'some kind of monster'. Perhaps she is not so sure as Isaac is about the goodness of God and is giving way to irrational fears. The mother of St Bernard had such a time of depression when she was carrying him, and she too imagined she was going to give birth to a monster—till a wise confessor

21

assured her that she was going to give birth indeed to a little dog who would bark so mightily against all the enemies of the Church that they would be too terrified to fight!

So she went to inquire of the Lord, we are told. Many commentators think that this means Rebekah consulted some priest at a local oracle. We may be sure that there were innumerable fortune-tellers and witch doctors and mediums everywhere in that world. Most of them were thoroughly bad. But even in such a world, it is possible that God had those who knew his mind and will. We have to remember how one of these local priests had been used by God to bless Abraham (Gen. 14.18ff.). But, indeed, Rebekah's 'inquiring of the Lord' can mean that she herself has learned to pray very much as Abraham and Isaac prayed. Such prayer is a 'pouring out of the heart' in its sorrows and troubles to God (Ps. 42.4; Ps. 62.8). The Psalmists often show us the way they did it (cf., e.g., Ps. 51; Ps. 88; Ps. 103).

The oracle of birth and strife

We can think of several different ways in which the famous oracle may have come to Rebekah. If she consulted some local shrine, it may have been simply spoken to her in the way we have it, by the priest or wise man in charge. If she went directly to God in prayer, then we can suppose that, as oracles came directly from God to privileged people like Abraham and to the prophets of Israel, so one came to this praying mother-to-be. It is handed on to us here as a short poem:

> *Two nations are in your womb,*
> *and two peoples, born of you, shall be divided;*
> *the one shall be stronger than the other,*
> *the elder shall serve the younger* (v. 23).

The message is immediately comforting and encouraging. It

clears away from her mind any thought that she is going to receive a shock at what will come from her womb. The commotion within her, she is told, is simply a sign of the vigour of two healthy children. She is going to have a successful labour.

But at the same time, the oracle brings news to disturb not Rebekah only, but also all women who will follow her in giving birth to their children even within the most select circles of church life. Rebekah at this time is a quiet, pious, God-fearing woman. She hates strife, abhors war and bloodshed. But now she is told by the divine oracle that she is carrying in her womb two boys who are each going to take part in the founding of a different people, and that their two nations will develop each in its own way to engage within the world's bitterly fought international strife. *Your issue will be two rival peoples* is the translation of the Jerusalem Bible (v. 23).

Her coming paradise, then, seems threatened by an evil to which she herself, in the service of God and even against her own will, is going to give birth. She must be disturbed at this announcement, even though she cannot see far into the future. She is, after all, one of the first mothers of God's 'chosen race', Abraham's family, God's new and splendid Church to come! In her married life with her husband she has experienced something of the 'blessing' and new life promised to the world in the new age-to-come. He and she have lived for the promise, and have remained separate from the outside world with its strife and evil. Can she not expect that the offspring of her marriage will be lifted above all the worst expectations that must attend human birth in this world? Will her very children at birth not give signs of a new light in their infant minds, and a new kind of life stirring in their natural beings—to pass on henceforth within this world as natural a propensity for good as there is a natural propensity for evil?

23

FROM ONE GENERATION TO ANOTHER

Privilege and responsibility

If her happiness seems to have a distant cloud over it, she surely must be overwhelmed by the privilege that is now to come to her. God is giving her the desires of her heart. She matters, now, not only to her husband, not only personally to God, but to the world around her and its affairs. This country girl from away back in Paddan-aram, so much confined to the tents of her husband, is now at the centre of the world's life and destiny. *Two nations*! Each of these children she is carrying is meant for greatness in making history. In giving birth and fulfilling the tasks of motherhood, she is mighty in the hand of God!

In her joy she reminds us of Hannah, who for years suffered privately in heart because of the low standard of moral life in her nation, the hypocrisy and deadness of the priesthood, and who, if she had been a man, would have become a prophet calling for reform. But all she could do was to pray, and suffer! Yet God heard her prayer for a child who would put things right, and she gave birth to Samuel, who under God was destined to save his nation. We have recorded for us the cry of exultation she uttered when she knew that she was pregnant after years of waiting:

> My heart exults in the Lord;
> . . . because I rejoice in thy salvation . . .
> The bows of the mighty are broken,
> but the feeble gird on strength.
> . . . He raises up the poor from the dust;
> . . . to make them sit with princes
> and inherit a seat of honour.
> . . . The adversaries of the Lord shall be
> broken in pieces. (1 Sam. 2.1, 4, 8, 10)

How wonderful it is that when God is planning the new and healthier beginnings with which he often interrupts and improves our human life, he plants the seed of these new beginnings within the processes of human birth, working in such a way as we read of here. One of the psalmists meditated on how close God had been to him all his days, guiding and interfering with even his secret thoughts, and he acknowledged that all this work of God's grace in him began both in the 'mind of God before he was born, and in the womb of his mother when God fashioned each of his members' (Ps. 139). Rebekah in her own way has had such thoughts, and they have helped her.

But she is warned while she is strengthened. Her privilege increases her responsibility and she has all the more difficult a task. The potential for strife instead of for blessing will be there even when the children are born. These boys are to be *two peoples, going their own ways from birth*! (v. 23 in the NEB translation). Here are potentially the seeds of disaster, sorrow and death. The conflict that she will find taking place on her lap and on her nursery floor can become that which ends on a bloody battlefield adding to the misery of mankind instead of saving from it.

But the call to privilege implies that she can overcome in the responsibility. God has already promised that she will not be mocked in answer to her prayer for a child who will bring a blessing and not a curse into this world's life. He will continue to answer her prayer as she faithfully goes on seeking by love, watchfulness, patience, teaching, warning, encouragement, fairness, tears and joy to help each to turn from his *own ways*, so that here there can be two nations in conflict for the service of God.

Original sin and new birth

We can think more deeply with this oracle than Rebekah could possibly have done, for we can interpret it now in the light of the whole of the Old Testament and of the New. It reminds us that even those born with all the potential for the service of God and mankind that comes from living in the heart of the Church and the Christian family are also born with all the potential of what we call 'original sin'.

There is in all human beings an inclination to live a life that is warped, self-centred, directed away from God, following desires that spoil our humanity and bring us into irreconcilable conflict with others who stand in our way. We tend, unless we are changed and reborn, to make this way of life a habitual part of ourselves. But this is not really something we acquire by learning and imitating others. It is something we bring with us at our birth. One of the psalmists puts the truth this way: 'Behold, I was brought forth in iniquity, and in sin did my mother conceive me' (Ps. 51.5).

'What causes wars, and what causes fightings among you?' asks James in his epistle. In answer, he speaks of the 'passions that war in your members'—or (as the Jerusalem Bible puts it) 'the desires fighting inside your own selves' (James 4.1). May it not be a clue to the meaning of this incident that Rebekah, with all her dedication to God, her great hopes and desires in his service, is also passing on to her children what she herself received through her parents when she received her human nature? Luther therefore described what Rebekah was bringing forth into her home as 'the same strife that took place between Cain and Abel, and the descendants of the serpent and the seed of the woman'. None of us can escape it or escape responsibility for it as it develops in each new generation and continues to pollute the stream of human history.

If we are justified in reading all this into the oracle given to Rebekah we must at the same time turn to another oracle given before the birth of another child:

Do not be afraid, Mary, for you have found favour with God. And behold, you will conceive in your womb and will bear a son . . . The Holy Spirit will come upon you,

26

and the power of the Most High will overshadow you; therefore the child to be born will be called holy, the Son of God (Luke 1.30-5).

Here is a birth different from and apart from all others; the birth of One who comes by the grace and power of God to bring no evil into the world, to concede nothing at any time to its temptations or evil ways but always to overcome. By his birth and life, death and resurrection, and the giving of his Spirit, he is able to reverse the transmission and spread of innate sin and thus of death from generation to generation by which our human life has been cursed. 'For as by one man's disobedience many were made sinners, so by one man's obedience many will be made righteous' (Rom. 5.19).

Our ensuing study will show us how, with a promise of such things to come, only partially enjoyed by Rebekah and her husband in their day, they struggled and failed, struggled again, succeeded at times and then failed again, yet by faith sought to please God and live by his grace in their time. Their struggles will show us more clearly where we too must struggle; their failure will show us where we have no excuse for not succeeding. Their successes are meant to assure us of greater success.

4

Esau and Jacob—I

GENESIS 25.24-8

The giving of a name

The natural make-up of these two boys is briefly outlined. The parents commemorated their birth when they named them. They called the first-born 'Esau', which meant a 'hairy covering'—the boy was born *red, all his body like a hairy mantle* (v. 25). In giving Esau this name they did not look ahead to the kind of character he would develop, for no indication was given of traits, good or bad.

With the second child it was otherwise. When he was born *his hand had taken hold of Esau's heel* (v. 26). They gave him the name 'Jacob', a name which could mean 'He takes by the heel'. The name 'Jacob' was therefore ominous and prophetic—though when the parents gave it they probably did not realize it. It can mean: 'He comes from behind! He takes people unawares! He tricks!' Jacob, all his life, till God took him forcibly in hand and radically changed him, was to live up to this name. He was to try by his cunning to manoeuvre even God into his plans!

His own early personal history was to make the name all the more uncomplimentary. To be called a 'Jacob' was like being called a 'Quisling' in our own century. Generations later the prophet Hosea surveyed the history of Jacob's direct successors—the tribe of Ephraim who descended from Joseph, Jacob's favourite son, whose twins received a special blessing from Jacob. They liked to be thought of as his special children, and the prophet in sheer sarcasm called them 'Jacob' in contrast to the southern tribes of 'Judah'. They were stubborn, untrustworthy and bent on going their

28

own ways. Hosea traced this tendency in their nature back to the birth of their ancestor of whom they were so proud: 'The Lord . . . will punish Jacob according to his ways . . . In the womb he took his brother by the heel, and in his manhood he strove with God' (Hos. 12.2-3). A recent commentator on Hosea, James L. Mays, sums up his accusation: 'Jacob's tricky career began before his birth . . . to the brother one was bound by closest ties of customary obligation, but Jacob violated the loyalty due his brother in the first sphere of his existence.'

Natural selection and variety in the Kingdom of God

As the two boys grew up, contrasting and opposite natural inclinations developed in each which bring them at times into open conflict: *Esau was a skilful hunter, a man of the field, while Jacob was a quiet man, dwelling in tents* (v. 27). G. von Rad comments on this verse helpfully:

As they grew up, the boys lived completely separated from each other, for they personified two ways of life typical of Palestine, which at that time was more wooded: that of the hunter and that of the shepherd. These two groups encountered each other particularly at the borders of civilization. From the viewpoint of cultural history the hunter is, of course, the older; the shepherd appeared only after a certain deforestation and working of the soil. But they lived for a long time contemporaneously and encountered each other especially on the borders of civilization in the East. They were unable to achieve a real symbiosis because of the profound difference in their needs. The relationship was in general rather tense. In any event, the roving and more uncultured hunter was a sinister person for the settled shepherd in more cultivated conditions.

This little section of our present chapter reminds us, then, that within this new family of God that is now appearing on earth, it is ordinary human nature, unsanctified, that is transmitted from parent to child; and every variety of human nature is to become incorporated here. God has no favourite types that he wants specially to set aside and cultivate. The town man, the country man, the business man, the mystical dreamer—all are valid. He is not only the God of Abraham, the courageous mystical pioneer. He wills to work also with Isaac, ordinary, conservative and retiring; with Esau, a brash and restless sportsman; and with Jacob, steady and clever, but cunning and manipulative. We are reminded of the extraordinary variety of different types of people whom Jesus gathered around him when he chose the twelve apostles. The inclusion of Jacob also reminds us that God never rejects anybody who begins badly—the 'difficult' child!

Parental folly

There is great potential in this family! They can enrich each other and broaden each other's lives. Yet things will never be easy with two such boys. It will require all the resources of wisdom, patience, love of both parents, united together and praying together, to keep control and to win success in the end. Holding together such a family will require from each parent an effort to see each particular child as a special gift of God to be held with care, an attempt to be fair always to both and to make each feel at home with them.

Instead, we read the fateful verse: *Isaac loved Esau, because he ate of his game; but Rebekah loved Jacob* (v. 28). The parents fail to provide the background of justice on which all true community and family life must be founded. They each champion a favourite; they allow the boys to divide them. As a result they further divide the boys and break apart what they are meant to unite. Isaac especially is blamed for carelessly demonstrating his partisanship for

Esau when the boy comes home from hunting with venison. Jacob grows up to realize that nothing he does can please his father as Esau does. Rebekah tries to compensate and complicates affairs. Of course the venison is a trivial matter! But within the family where human hearts are sensitive, there are often no trivial matters.

Premature decision

The situation is made even more bitter and complicated by another factor which entered the minds of both parents and so of both children far earlier than it should have done. The phrase *Isaac loved Esau* has overtones.

In the book of Deuteronomy the word 'love' used within the context of family life is linked up with the allocation by a parent of the birthright. Where a family is divided by the personal bias of the father, one side being 'loved' the other 'unloved', he is warned that he must not allow his 'love' for one side and his dislike for the other to influence his judgement about who should have preference in the passing on of the family birthright (Deut. 21.15-17; cf. NEB. Paul uses this passage in connection with the Jacob-Esau story).

That *Isaac loved Esau* can with justice, then, be taken to read that he is determined to make Esau not only heir to the double portion of his estate—his right as first-born—but also the heir to the blessing that will connect him directly with the promise made to Abraham and invest him with the responsibility of passing it on. That *Rebekah loved Jacob* means in the same way that Jacob is not just the favourite in her human affections but her candidate to train and ordain to be primarily responsible for receiving the promise made to Abraham.

As we will read later, in the end Isaac's determination to give this blessing as well as the birthright to Esau, over against Rebekah's determination that Jacob, and not Esau, should have it, will finally break up the home; but the division begins here as the boys are growing up. The narrator has deliberately arranged his story in such a way as to show that the decision of each parent was unjustifiable and premature.

5

Esau and Jacob—II

GENESIS 25.29-34

The enigmatic oracle

We have seen that the whole of the early home life of Esau and Jacob was overshadowed, especially for Isaac and Rebekah, by the question of who was to become direct heir to the promise made by God to Abraham and his successors and thus responsible for its transmission and fulfilment. We have suggested, too, that Isaac and Rebekah both dwelt too long upon the meaning of the oracle given to Rebekah at the time of their birth. It had said: 'Two peoples, born of you, shall be divided; The one shall be stronger than the other, The elder shall serve the younger' (Gen. 25.23).

What did it mean? As to who was first-born there could be no doubt. But who was referred to as the *younger* who would serve the *elder* and what did it mean to 'serve'? Each parent mistakenly tried to understand the oracle before history unfolded its meaning: as a result, each interpreted it differently. Rebekah took the more obvious meaning. Surely it claimed for her Jacob ultimate precedence. He was the 'younger' and his being 'served' must imply God's favour in this matter of the blessing. Isaac, as Luther pointed out, took a more subtle interpretation. He argued that the struggle in which the 'younger' prevailed had already taken place within the mother's womb. There, potentially, Jacob was the elder but Esau was thrust into pre-eminence by God, even though Jacob had tried to trip him up as God thrust him out!

The reader is meant to notice that this oracle was originally uttered enigmatically. It had deliberate reserve and ambiguity. It left matters quite open—it was an appeal to both parents to wait. To leave history to bring its true meaning to light. It was a promise that history, in the end—but only *in the end*—would clearly manifest God's decision about these two boys. God did not will that the parents should know the tasks he had destined either child to fulfil, or which he would choose. Why indeed, in the end, should he not choose both?

An enigmatic happening

A story is told of an early happening. It reminds us that there was no justification early in the lives of these boys for any decision to be made about one or the other from the human point of view.

One day Esau comes home desperately hungry after hunting. He has been out for many hours and has caught nothing. It could seem to be merely a coincidence that Jacob is there with a meal ready-cooked. But his behaviour suggests that it was a trap laid carefully in the hope that things would happen exactly as they did. It is only a dish of lentils that Jacob has cooking, but it has been prepared with great skill. The colour and the smell are exactly those that appeal to and catch Esau's appetite, and make him feel even more hungry. Indeed it looks and smells so good that Esau, a little extravagantly, is led to confess that his life depends on having it—and at that very moment, Jacob, waiting for

33

a sign from Esau, has his bargain in his mind, and he is wondering how far he is going to be able to go.

Esau raises his hopes: *Let me eat some of that red pottage, for I am famished!* (v. 30). Von Rad says that the word here for 'eat' means 'gulp down'. Another commentator suggests that he thinks it was his favourite 'blood-soup'. Jacob therefore believes he can start the unholy bargaining: *Not till you sell me your rights as the first-born* (v. 31 NEB). Esau further betrays himself by talking as if he were on the verge of real collapse: *I am at death's door. What use is my birth-right to me?* (v. 32 NEB). At this point Jacob, probably spilling the soup as he eagerly and liberally pours it out with his excited, shaky hand, believes he can clinch everything by extracting an oath from his crazy brother before he tastes it: *Not till you answer* (v. 33 NEB). Esau, on the spur of the moment, swears the oath demanded of him.

What are we to make of this story, told of this stage in the adolescence of these two boys? Those who deal only with the superficial aspects of the Bible and find a basis in folklore for these tales in Genesis regard it as a story written for its times, illustrating the dependence, in a crisis, of the hunting and roving type of man on the man who lives by agriculture and sheep-breeding in a more settled state of existence.

Of course these stories are all so relevant to life under different conditions that we can give the tale a number of other convincing superficial and allegorical applications. Is it not equally a story written for today? Jacob is, of course, the expert both in market research and in advertising. He knows what his public wants, the colour of the food and the smell that pleases, and can advertise it in such a way that the client begins to feel that his very life depends on having it at this very moment! It is a tribute to Jacob's skill in doing this that the ingredients of what he is offering are worthless—a few lentils—but with his skill he has made them seem worth a kingdom! Esau of course represents typically the gullible public, undiscerning, easily fooled and living always on a superficial level with low tastes.

But the story is recorded here as a history rather than as an allegory. (It often happens that true history has a multitude of symbolic overtones.) It is a family story about the boys treasured and handed on probably by Rebekah and often told by her during the long period of loneliness she had to live through after Jacob was finally exiled from home, illustrating just the kind of thing he was always up to!

On our first reading through this story, however, we find difficulty in judging which of the two we despise most. Probably most of us will prefer Esau. At least he was a good sporting man! Jacob is an ugly character. Even our low standards in sportsmanship today would condemn him. Yet when we think it over, Esau shows up badly too. He had pretended all his life to his doting and trusting father that he loved and lived for God's blessing. But here it is clearly shown that it had all been hypocrisy. He had no compunction beforehand in making the bargain, and not a twinge of conscience after it: *he ate and drank and went his way* (v. 34).

By all the moral and spiritual standards we ourselves can apply, then, the incident leaves us, as onlookers, in the dark about the great question: which boy?

God sees—and decides!

While we ourselves are left thus in perplexity, God was not left in any doubt. The writer of the story adds a note at the end of it about his belief that this incident clinched the matter in the eyes of God himself: *Thus Esau despised his birthright* (v.34). Many of the details of the story may go against Jacob, but in the narrator's opinion no hope can remain for a man who in an emergency can reveal as Esau did that in his heart he despises the best that God can give! God sees it all at that moment—in Esau! For here Esau

35

throws off all disguise and makes clear before his maker what his decision about the ultimate things in life really is.

The writer of the Epistle to the Hebrews agrees with this view. He appeals to his readers to 'see that . . . none be immoral or irreligious like Esau, who sold his birthright for a single meal'. His appeal implies that only after this act was Esau rejected by God and failed to attain his grace, for he had made it impossible for God to use him in his service (Heb. 12.15-17). This incident, in his view, proved that Esau, though he later wept over what he had lost, by this final decision had no longer left in him any will to true repentance but could only weep self-centred tears. Because he had now orientated himself so deliberately away from God there could be no further hope for him.

The decision which God then made about these two boys came to light gradually as time went on. It was Jacob and not Esau who was to be changed, and to become Israel, a father of the people of God. But surely Esau too could have been changed and fitted into God's purpose. We find that Esau was completely rejected; the nation he founded became an enemy of the people of God and finally disappeared from the scene of human history.

A further enigma

A further enigma arises over the case of Esau and Jacob when we read other comments in the Bible about the story. The book of Malachi reminds us of the fact that it was not Esau's rejection of God but God's rejection of Esau that decided everything in the end. ' "Is not Esau, Jacob's brother," says the Lord, "yet I have loved Jacob but I have hated Esau; I have laid waste his hill country and left his heritage to jackals of the desert" ' (Mal. 1.3). The words 'love' and 'hate' are a slightly strong way of saying 'choose' and 'reject' (cf p. 31). In the New Testament, Paul quotes this saying of Malachi in a passage in which he teaches that

God 'hardens whomever he wills, and has mercy on whomever he wills'. The rejection of Esau, then, is an illustration of the freedom of God's perfect, wise and loving will. Paul in this passage affirms that God made this choice between Jacob and Esau before either was born (Rom. 9.6-18).

So we have the story viewed from two points of view even within the Bible! We have those passages that put the blame on Esau for his own decision about God himself—especially the decision he made at the moment he sold his birthright. And we have those which remind us that God always decides unerringly beforehand—and knows what he is going to decide. We have the story interpreted from the point of view of our own free will and also interpreted from the point of view of God's predestination of everything that happened.

Comfort and warning

Even though we cannot logically work out which side the Bible supports on this matter of God's predestination and our free will we must try to hold both sides together in our faith and in our attempts to live the Christian life.

It is a great comfort to us to reflect that God made his decision about us before we were born. It was not our choice of God or our goodness that determined what we are and where we stand today before him, but his choice of us. Before our eyes saw the light of day, his were upon us, controlling and influencing what happened to us and seeking to bring us to himself. His was the stronger hand when there was a conflict within us and we wanted to go loose and free. He prepared all our blessings and our good fortune. He prepared our trials and sufferings. He worked everything together for good. If we can grasp this truth, it gives us the firm assurance that he will finish his work come what may, always overruling our wills and our mistakes.

But Esau, even though he was in the hands of God, obviously rejected God, and we must not lull ourselves into a false security and forget the warnings given to us from this story about Esau despising his birthright. Should there not be a 'fear and trembling' in our lives as we think of the privilege it is to have our birthright, to belong to God in this way, and of the cost of our privilege as we see it in the cross of Christ? 'See that . . . no one be . . . like Esau!' (Heb. 12.16). It is a false security that does not have in it some element of fear and trembling. So solemn is this warning that people can be driven to despair if they forget Paul's teaching and emphasize only this text: might I myself not have entered by my own weak free will the same unforgiveable and irretrievable condition as Esau?

If we are worried in any way as to whether or not we may have drifted into, or decided ourselves into, the unforgiveable and irretrievable state of mind we find in Esau, then we have not done so. For we are still concerned about God, in a way that Esau was not at all concerned. The door to his service and his mercy is open for all of us who are willing to hear his call to service and his offer of mercy. It is open till we close it from within—only from within—and do not wish it open. Let us remember that Jacob was there alongside Esau, as bad as Esau ever was with only one difference—he would have trembled before the possibility of being cast away by God!

God alone can know!

When anyone has slammed the door from within, as Esau did, his or her act in doing so is so deep-seated and thus hidden that no one in the outside world can tell at the time what has been done. On this matter of who is elected by God and who is rejected, the Bible answers that God alone can see, and God alone can know. 'The Lord knows those who are his' (2 Tim. 2.19).

Cleavages always appear in Christian churches, congregations, families. We cannot always avoid them. There are, after all, contradictory schools of thought. Sometimes for conscience's sake people feel they have to choose ways of living that tend to separate them from those who prefer other ways. It would not be life in the real world if we had no strong controversies over our interpretation of the Bible and the gospel. These become very deep and seriously disruptive only when people of one school of thought begin to think of themselves as elected and of the others as rejected, and when parents begin to make such deeply penetrating judgements about children, or children about parents. Then indeed we have the beginnings of an alienation that can have bitter ultimate consequences. We find this in the story of Isaac's family where he and Rebekah dared to make such premature judgements.

Both Rebekah and Isaac thought the decision made was the correct interpretation of an oracle of God; and we, too, can base our utter rejection of another in the name of God on our own partial interpretation of biblical texts. But both Isaac and his wife were motivated by their own partiality to an extent far greater than they knew. So today what we can call non-theological factors can play a larger part in our judgements about others than we imagine. We would do well always to heed the wise advice of Paul: 'Do not pronounce judgement before the time, before the Lord comes, who will bring to light the things now hidden in darkness and will disclose the purposes of the heart. Then every man will receive his commendation from God' (1 Cor. 4.5). We have enough divisions already without hardening ourselves in doubtful ones.

6

Isaac—By Himself

GENESIS 26.1–33

The ordinary man

We already know something about Isaac. We have watched him rise to the occasion when his wife was troubled in mind. We have just watched him make a rather tragic and common mistake in a home problem that was to bring deep tragedy into his later family life. We now have a whole chapter devoted to him by himself. It shows how he faced up to his limitations and difficulties in public life. It pays a tribute to certain of his personal qualities.

He is different from his father and from his son Jacob, except in his religious faith and perhaps in appearance, and he plays an entirely different role in the family history than does either of them.

This chapter is intended to pay tribute to the man. He may not have had outstanding gifts and his home life does not succeed in impressing us as exemplary. Nevertheless in spite of some failures he overcame his limitations, registered his protest and made his mark on the events of the world around him. His achievements, too, deserve mention alongside those of Abraham and Jacob and Joseph.

Tradition can make ordinary men great by what it does to them and the opportunities it gives them of upholding it. But an ordinary man can also enrich the tradition itself by adding to it the things that he alone can exemplify and do.

Rowing the boat

The Church has always had its great pioneers. When their boat was under difficulties on the sea of Galilee the disciples saw Jesus walking on the water. Peter challenged him: 'Lord if it is you, bid me come to you on the water' (Matt. 14.28). He heard the command 'Come'; he ventured, he walked. It was an outstanding feat of initiative, daring and faith.

It was Peter's privilege to be called to do the daring, outstanding thing. The others were not called to emulate him. But they rowed the boat, for the boat had to be there to take Peter back when he was finished. One does the outstanding thing; eleven do the regular thing and have to accept the limitations of their place and their work. Otherwise there can be no background against which the daring act can be seen as extraordinary, no basis for its accomplishment. Isaac was one of life's oarsmen.

He is told at the beginning of his career that he will have to reconcile himself to quite narrow boundaries in his range of God's service. *The Lord appeared to him, and said, 'Do not go down to Egypt; dwell in the land of which I shall tell you. Sojourn in this land . . .'* (vv. 2–3).

We are not told why Isaac is so rigidly restricted as to the sphere of his activity and experience. It may be that God can see some weakness in his character that makes him unwilling to subject the man to the temptations of a world bigger and yet more dangerous than the one he is confined to. We are told to pray 'lead us not into temptation'. For each of us there are spheres of life into which we can either drift or direct ourselves but where we could not stand up to the pressures.

There may be another reason why Isaac is to be limited. In the lives of these early patriarchs patterns are being created, standards are being set for the kind of piety God is going to expect from those who are to be his people. Certain aspects of Abraham's life of faith make him a model for all of us at times. But only few of us will be able to follow him to his greatest heights. So likewise Jacob's example will only sometimes appeal strongly to some of us. But where Abraham and Jacob become somewhat lofty, Isaac at his best and in his truest response to the Word of God will be a model for many.

We find people like him reappearing again and again in the Bible. He is there, surely, in Obadiah, that steady and reliable layman who was not so outstandingly gifted or courageous as Elijah or Elisha but who nevertheless did an important job (1 Kings 18). He is there also in Baruch, Jeremiah's secretary, who probably was not much more than a good scribe but to whom we owe the preservation of Jeremiah's writings. He was there in the companions of Paul, who seemed not to be able to function well unless he had one or two around him.

What matters is that, like Isaac, we should know that we are called to be where we are—within the limitations we are sometimes tempted to fret about; in the routine family job which no one knows is so hard as we do, and no one thanks us for doing; on the sick bed, all the day, weeks on end; in the insignificant little church which people pass by to go to the big and popular one. We surely find fellowship with Isaac when we hear him told to stay exactly where he is, as an act of obedience, requiring before God strong self-discipline and total self-sacrifice. To Abraham the word of God came: 'Get out'; and he went. To Isaac the same word of God said: *Sojourn in this land*. The obedience that each gave cost the same!

Sounding the depths

As a youngster when his father took him to the mountain and bound him in order to offer him as a sacrifice to God, Isaac must have entered the same great depths of isolated suffering before God as his father did—even though he was less able to understand everything that was at stake in the happening (Gen. 22; cf. *Abraham*, pp. 126-38). Twice in this present chapter within a fairly short space of time, it is recorded that there happened to Isaac, too, exactly what happened to Abraham at other great moments of his life with God: *The Lord appeared to him and said* . . . (vv. 2, 24). The intimate conversation involved God sharing with him his concern for his purposes and promises, and giving him the assurance: 'Fear not.' Abraham never got, never asked for more.

The great masters of the spiritual life, like St John of the Cross, have laboured to chart for us the mystic way to God. They tell us about meditation, then about contemplation, and they report to us that at the summit of a genuine experience of God there is what they call the 'dark night of the soul' when all our thinking, our feeling, our will to probe the unseen and to live before God seem to be negated, for in the presence of God such things must themselves become shattered. Generations of followers who have read such mystic writings have benefited by their pioneering experiences and their showing of the way.

But, if we could have encouraged him to speak to us and to others, who could tell us more about the dark night of the soul, and living with God, than Isaac? He may look much less important, much more naïve, not so practical and capable as his father. He may not be so articulate as others or so able to frame or even to understand a theological statement. He is the type who would probably not come through very well in the psychological tests we sometimes use today to determine a person's fitness for the ministry of the gospel. He is not the type to have been made the chairperson in important church committees. But before God he hears and sees and feels as profoundly as God desires his presence to be heard and seen and felt.

Are we not meant to see this depth of experience as closely connected with his faithfulness to his ordinary vocation?

Where the one is, the other will be. Paul in one place underlines this truth. There is no need for all people when they become Christians to forsake the ordinary tasks of life, or to try to cut loose from the earthly vocation in order somehow to become more useful and near to God. 'Each one, my friends, is to remain before God, in the condition in which he received his call' (1 Cor. 7.24 NEB)—the ordinary man, Isaac, remaining where he is, but always 'before God'! Who can seek anything higher or deeper in religious experience than this?

Perhaps if we want to know more about communion with God we should try to get nearer to some of the Isaacs around us to encourage them, perhaps in a Bible study or prayer group, to tell us what they know about God's nearness, faithfulness and help. John Bunyan owed his first experience of God to what he received in conversation with three or four godly women whom he first overheard talking about their faith as they sat in the sunshine. The great early Methodist preacher John Harvey found a new creed and a message to preach in a conversation with an unlettered ploughman. Luther, on this chapter, complains that the Church for its knowledge of God seeks to find so much amongst the writings of St Anthony and St Bernard, who had no familiarity with either women or cattle—whereas God is trying to teach us something of his word through Isaac, of whom little is related except that 'he was born to his father Abraham, begot children, tended cattle, and wandered about in various regions'!

Unwanted publicity and unsought prosperity

The publicity that comes to Isaac in Gerar is hard to bear, for he is of a retiring nature. But he cannot help it that Rebekah, possibly like Sarah before her, looks foreign, striking and beautiful. The men around are interested, and no doubt suggest to Isaac that they date her. Stupidly and faithlessly he remembers what his father did in a like situation (Gen. 16 and 20)—and his father had come through all right! He says, 'she is my sister' (v. 4), for he is afraid for his life. Nobody believes it. Such an abject, ordinary-looking fellow—brother of a woman like her! His answer increases the public attention. People start to spy on him till no less a man than King Abimelech, in curiosity, looks out on them from his palace window and catches them!

Isaac was *fondling Rebekah his wife* (v. 8). The phrase used could yield the translation as in the NEB: they were *laughing together*, with a laughter that implied some intimacy. Luther calls it 'some conjugal silliness . . . becoming to this kind of life'. There was nothing serious about it. He seizes on the fact that the name 'Isaac' actually means laughter (Gen. 21.6); 'Isaac was Isaacing', he says, 'the laughing, friendly and lovable man being friendly with his wife, conducting himself like the real Isaac . . . with the unconcern and confidence of a married man.'

The consequences for such as Isaac are painful in the extreme. He is summoned to appear before the king, and no doubt many others hear him being gently twitted now that all the public speculation has been authoritatively ended: *So she is your wife, is she?* (v. 9 NEB). For a short time Isaac becomes the most publicized man in the area and the story is the biggest joke of the day. His old man, too, the Philistines remember, had done the same kind of thing! Why, in spite of it, the king gave both a favoured status nobody could understand.

As they watch him more, they begin to notice his astonishing prosperity: *And Isaac sowed in that land, and reaped in the same year a hundredfold. The Lord blessed him, and the man became rich, and gained more and more until he became very wealthy* (vv. 12-13). This prosperity has come as much unsought by Isaac as was the publicity. He is now high in the king's favour. He is protected and privileged, and God has enriched him.

More than envy?

We can attribute what happened now simply to jealousy. Even though there was no real fault, the Philistines *envied him* (v. 14) and began to persecute him in order to drive him out (vv. 15-16, 18, 20). They complained to the king as a body—just as Daniel's contemporaries in Babylon turned against him (Dan. 6.16).

But in the light of all the circumstances and the whole subsequent history of the people of God we are justified in seeing this as the beginning of something much more complex and sinister than simple envy. What began here in Gerar has broken out time and again since in history. We call it anti-semitism. It broke out in Egypt in the frenzy of persecution against the Israelites led by Pharaoh and worked up by false propaganda (Exod. 1-12). It was repeated in Persia (cf. Esther 1 ff.). It often became a characteristic of the Gentile's treatment of the Jew throughout European history, and it found its climax in the holocaust under Hitler.

Some people try to explain it psychologically and rationally. Might it not be *really* due to envy or to the normally explicable suspicion of a foreigner and stranger—especially of a wealthy one where the source of the wealth is secret and therefore to be suspected? The strict 'apartness' into which Isaac's unique faith forced him at the time did not help. His detractors could spread false stories about undesirable secret religious rites.

But the irrationality of the complaint and the persecution is emphasized. That the Philistine king should seek to drive out a petty and peace-loving chieftain like Isaac because he was a threat to public order and safety in the region (v. 16) was as big a joke as his fondling of his wife. There seems to be no good reason for anti-semitism except that people on this earth seem to be especially easily stirred up to hate that which God has decided especially to use and bless, and perhaps we see the true nature of our anti-semitic tendencies revealed in what broke out around Jesus at the cross.

The search for peace

But it comes as a shock to Isaac to realize that for no reason all those around him seem determined on his ruin. They not only spread slanders and manufactured false complaints; they strike determinedly at his life-line—his water supply. As he is compelled now to move around, they block up one after another of the wells he digs—'a custom among the ancients', comments Calvin, 'if they wished to involve anyone in ruin'. The birds of the air had nests and the foxes had holes but Isaac was to be driven out. The king had been one of his father's trusted friends, but for a time he connives at what is going on and Isaac is utterly defenceless and friendless (vv. 17-20).

During this period of misery, as the narrator points out, Isaac followed his father's footsteps and *dug again the wells of water which had been dug in the days of Abraham his father* (v. 18). Preachers have often taken this text to allegorize on the fact that Isaac had not the originality to cut out any new paths for himself but was content to follow in every respect his father's ways in thought, customs and personal habit. Why not? He is in search of peace and he seeks first the protection and help of God who never failed his father. He expects to find strength and relief in doing what that great man of God did before him—by getting back, as it were, to where Abraham had been. The situation around him is too critical for him not to fall back on the certainties he already has. Isaac's behaviour is the kind advised to a later generation by a prophet addressing his restless and fearful countrymen in Babylon at one stage of their exile: 'Harken to me, you who pursue deliverance, You who seek the Lord; Look to the rock from which you were hewn, and to the quarry from

47

which you were digged. Look to Abraham your father and to Sarah who bore you' (Isa. 51.1-2).

How much Isaac prayed verbally we are not told, but his whole life at least was a dumb cry for help to the God of his father Abraham; and it was precisely in that role that God answered. Somehow the tension ceases. The persecutors seem to grow tired and, as an assurance to Isaac that his prayers have been answered he has his final great experience at Beersheba: *And the Lord appeared to him . . . and said, 'I am the God of Abraham your father; fear not, for I am with you and will bless you and multiply your descendants for my servant Abraham's sake'* (v. 24). The whole incident is a charter for those of us who fail to find satisfaction and strength in new paths, new directions and new ways, who are perhaps tired and disappointed, are encouraged at least to start again to read, study, pray, seek, ask, knock, exactly in the place where our fathers and mothers did before us.

Isaac, we have to notice, offers no retaliation. When he is persecuted in one place he moves on; in the next place, again he moves on. It is the wisest course and he can afford to do this, with such a God.

As a second sign that God is with him, Isaac is made the subject of another of those frequent miracles that so often changed things in the Bible when God's people were in trouble. Something happens to a king somewhere—a vision, or a dream, or a thought, or a change of heart or an accident. Anyway the ruler finally changes his mind and this alters everything for the one below who has been crying to God in trouble. Abimelech here suddenly becomes friendly again, anxious to make everything up (vv 26-31). There is no explanation but the one that applies again and again in the history of Israel: 'The king's heart is a stream of water in the hand of the Lord; he turns it wherever he will' (Prov. 21.1).

7

The Family Crisis—Isaac

GENESIS 26.34-27.4

Bitterness and danger

When Esau was forty years old, he took to wife Judith the daughter of Beeri the Hittite, and Basemath, the daughter of Elon the Hittite, and they made life bitter for Isaac and Rebekah (26.34).

Abraham had been called by God to sacrifice, and to venture everything in order to create a people who would be free for ever from the heathenism of the world of his day. But now two women, deeply committed to this very paganism, are installed at the heart of the life of the family Abraham had taught, under God, 'to keep the way of the Lord, by doing righteousness and justice' (Gen. 18.19). The two of them soon find themselves in direct conflict with the strange religion and the moral tradition of their new circle. They know, too, that their own husband, at heart, cares little for these things. We can well imagine the havoc they cause by their stubborn refusal to fit in, their subtle questioning of what they find going on around them.

It must be a bitter thought, indeed, to Isaac that this alien, undoubtedly divisive, and poisoning influence in his home was introduced by the willful decision of the favourite son for whom he feels so deeply responsible. Rebekah herself, on the woman's side of the house, comes up against the newcomers even more forcibly than Isaac. Knowing that she favours Jacob in matters of inheritance, they are from the start more readily prejudiced against her. Moreover, in the upper levels of the domestic administration, they are now two against one!

49

This new situation is, of course, as full of danger as it is of vexation and perplexity. Can a family circle as Isaac's now is, with such influences at its heart, retain the promise that it can teach the world about God? Here is a problem facing Isaac in his old age, which is more deeply rooted and complex than any he has had to face before. It is a reminder to us that it is often what happens in the last chapter of our book of life that determines everything that lies ahead, and that therefore we are never able to retire from our responsibility within the Kingdom of God.

The steps Isaac takes as he tries to face this problem, or rather as he refuses to face it, bring about a crisis in his own relationship with God—and the rest of the family become deeply involved, each with his or her own responsibility, in the sad affairs that follow.

And at home!

Before this last chapter of Isaac's story proceeds we are suddenly and quietly taken entirely away from Isaac's public life. The door to the home is shut, and everything now becomes entirely private to the family. It is here at home that Isaac has to make his most important decision before God—here at home, for it is here that destiny seems to be closer to each of us than elsewhere. It is precisely here that we are most sensitive to one another; it is here that, if we do not help each other, as we are intended to, we can hurt each other decisively—parents, children; children, parents; parents, each other; children, each other.

Here at home, of course, for years Isaac has felt that he has unusually great difficulties to cope with. His two boys have been fighters from infancy, strangely distrustful and jealous of each other. His wife radically disagrees with his own sincerely held conviction that Jacob can never have been marked out for future leadership within the family of God. The very circumstances of the birth of this second boy seemed against him. He is too treacherous to be trusted, too much wrapped up in himself, too calculating. Esau, the first-born, has always been Isaac's dear hope, and he has prayed many times that Rebekah will come to see that he has chosen rightly.

Rebekah has also felt, no less acutely, that the marriage trouble stemming from their division over Jacob is a tragedy. It would be some consolation if her husband could only see through Esau, as she has done for years, and admit that he has chosen the wrong boy. But even in their shared bitterness over the Hittite women, Isaac seems to remain as distant from her on this point as ever.

It is here at home, then, that Isaac and Rebekah in their pilgrimage come to their lowest point, their darkest valley, their place of trouble, tears and utter loneliness of heart.

The 'door of hope'

The situation is, however, meant to be seen as a situation of hope. It becomes very clear as this last story about Isaac develops that at this very time, with more pressure than he has ever exerted before in their personal lives, God is there, alertly watching over every detail of these pathetic family affairs. He is there ready to speak and intervene in a new, creative and decisive way.

Isaac could himself have realized that this was so, if he had stopped to consider carefully the new turn events around him were taking, and how this should affect his thinking about his past, present and future. If, for instance, he had thought seriously about the story of Abraham his father which he knew so well, he would have realized that it is always when things seem most hopeless, and when every possibility of new life and true fulfilment has disappeared from the human scene, that great things become possible with God (Gen. 18.14).

Moreover, he might have remembered that even Abraham

51

had had sometimes to concede that he had been wrong in his dreams and wishes about his son Ishmael, and that Sarah his wife, in opposing him, had been right (Gen. 21.9-12; cf. *Abraham*, pp. 111-14). Was it not time for Isaac now to recognize that the problem that divided him from Rebekah had cleared up? That Esau had disqualified himself beyond recovery? That she had been right and he had been wrong?

Within the bitterness and the danger there was opening up a new possible way for him to take—a God-given opportunity for reconciliation with his wife and with the truth. Could not he, the man of peace abroad, now bring the same peace to his home as he had won in public? Man and wife, together, he and Rebekah could at least have started out on the difficult new way, going step by step under the guidance of God.

The psalm-writer describes the pilgrims travelling to the holy feast in the temple of God. They meet dangers and joys, pass through trials and temptations on the way. He describes one of its stages: 'As they go through the valley of Baca, they make it a place of springs' (Ps. 84.6). The 'Valley of Baca' is the name for the valley of bitterness and trouble. It involves them in a wearisome trudge through hard black countryside. But this very place, to their hearts and minds, becomes a 'landscape with bubbling fountains and pasture', says a commentator (A. Weiser). 'The impossible and the improbable is here made possible and real: affliction is transformed into joy, hardship into rejoicing, weakness into strength.' Hosea, in the same strain, promises that God will make the 'Valley of Achor' (the valley of trouble) into a 'door of hope'—which, another commentator tells us, meant 'an entry into a life of promise, a future unlimited by the painful past' (Mays on Hos. 2.15).

Isaac must now look for such a door. He will be untrue to his father and to the meaning of what has come into the world through his father's work if he fails to believe that he will yet praise God for the bitterness (Ps. 42.5).

The unsurrendered mind

If Isaac is to find the door, however, he must first make the surrender; he must, as it were, be prepared to 'slay' Esau—his favourite son—before God, as his father Abraham was prepared to slay him, his favourite son, when called upon by God to do so. Isaac, less dramatically than Abraham but no less searchingly, is now being tested in his old age as to whether he too is prepared to surrender his will, his plans and hopes for the future. Can he rise to it and say—as Abraham in his last great trial said three times—simply 'Lord here I am' (Gen. 22.1, 7, 11)?

The lesson taught to Abraham that day on Mount Moriah (and Isaac himself was there at the time!) was simply: 'On the mount of the Lord it shall be provided' (Gen. 22.14), i.e. the way of hope will be opened as the surrender is made!

In many passages in the Bible the future of the people of God is shown to have depended on key people (and always there have been such people) simply making their personal surrender to God in their worst moments of despair and destitution. We can read of this situation with people like Samson (e.g. Judges 16.30), Samuel (1 Sam. 3.10), David (e.g. 1 Sam. 17.45; 2 Sam. 7.24; 2 Sam. 16.11-12), Isaiah (Isa. 6.8) and Jeremiah (Jer. 1.4-10); their outstanding leadership and influence in their day were due simply to their being able to say to God, especially when things were most difficult, 'Lord, here I am'.

We find it happening this way in the New Testament too—in Mary (Luke 1.38) and in Ananias of Damascus (Acts. 9.10) and Paul (Acts 22.10). And we find it embodied in the perfect life that came to its perfect expression in the prayer in Gethsemane: 'Nevertheless not my will, but thine!' (Luke 22.42).

Now is Isaac's opportunity. Let him make his self-offering in mind, in will and heart, and he will be shown the door of hope. God is there, waiting for his response so that the promises he has made can now be pushed through towards fulfilment. Yet at this point Isaac becomes one of the most abject and tragic figures in Scripture. Though he is utterly weak, almost overwhelmed, he is determined to work his own way through the family crisis before the end overtakes him. He will not admit himself beaten. He will play the last few cards in his miserable hand, in a desperate attempt to push things on in the way he has always thought God willed them.

Of course he has to become furtive in doing so. He hides his intentions and keeps himself apart from his wife. His secretiveness creates an atmosphere of suspicion in which one person begins to plot against the other, and one begins to spy on the other.

The plot

In those days, apparently, the law did not always determine that the son who was physically firstborn should have any priority in the disposition of a family inheritance. There was a recognized practice that a father on his death-bed, even with a last word, could name and bless the one he there and then appointed as his successor.

Isaac determines that in spite of Rebekah and Jacob, he will now endow Esau finally and officially with the birthright of the elder son, and that the 'blessing' which his father Abraham passed on to him will also go along with it. This will be done in an irrevocable and solemn act, in secret, between himself and his favourite. After it, he believes, there need be no more uncertainty or tension.

In order to have his way he has to take a course which seems both mean and cowardly. To avoid any danger of conflict he excludes both Rebekah and Jacob from what ought to be the most joyful, meaningful and united affair in the family history—the naming and blessing of the heir to the promise given by God to Abraham. Some commentators believe that Isaac's behaviour at this point betrays a degeneracy in his thought about God that contrasts sadly with what we were led to admire in Abraham. Has he become naïve enough to believe that by the mere utterance of a few formal words in a correct and legal ritualistic context he can determine the ultimate direction of a blessing from God? Does he now believe that a blessing will come more powerfully and effectively if the celebrant has been fortified and inspired by a good meal solemnly eaten beforehand? At any rate it is stupid of him to imagine that he can push his plan through so quietly and quickly that Rebekah will not come to be aware of what is taking place.

Yet the plan is deliberately thought out. It is not to be interpreted as the excusable act of one who has become in any way 'senile'. The whole story shows us that Isaac, though physically blind, has all his natural wits about him.

8

The Family Crisis—Rebekah

GENESIS 27.5-17

The example

However much Rebekah is to be condemned, she must nevertheless be allowed to stand out, in the circumstances in which she finds herself, as a shining example of how faith must always seek to act. Her husband, to whom God has given responsibility for leadership in the family, is playing the fool, acting unworthily and thwarting God's will. She herself therefore feels responsible—as a witness who cannot stand by and do nothing. She believes that the fulfilment of the promises of God will be at stake unless she acts. She feels herself called by God now to act alone and play the part. Did Abraham himself in his day not accept such lonely responsibility—and is she not meant to be a true daughter of Abraham? She has no thought for herself, but only for God, his Kingdom, her boy, and her husband too—who must be rescued from the results of his folly. Commentators criticize her for not waiting, but she feels she cannot wait. There is too much at stake at this very moment!

In all this we again see her as the forerunner of one of the greatest women who ever took part in Israel's history, whose life greatly influenced Mary the mother of our Lord. Hannah in her day was in the same position as Rebekah (1 Sam. 1–2). Everything was degenerating spiritually and morally and nobody except she seemed to care. The men around her who had responsibility in Church and state were incredibly stupid and unconcerned. The only decent priest was senile, and the others were disgusting. Her own husband couldn't see that much was wrong. She herself, she alone, felt that God had laid responsibility for the future of the nation on her shoulders, so that she should at least produce a son who could become a leader to save his people. But she was barren. She threw herself into a passion of prayer till God answered her. She certainly was wiser and more restrained than Rebekah. She went about things in a different way—but she imitated her great predecessor's faith.

Let us therefore fully recognize the greatness of the instinct that forced Rebekah into action. Can we not, like Hannah, take her today as an example not of method but of faith and zeal? Lay men and women are surely to be encouraged not to wait too long for an official lead, when they see a need around the church and nobody else concerned to meet it.

No wonder Luther praises Rebekah so much. She went about the affair 'with skill, ingenuity, and a very beautiful stratagem'. She influenced her son well. She and Jacob 'acted in a godly and saintly manner', for they 'had every right to despoil Esau'.

Bishop Hall bids us take note of her practical skill and thoroughness in the execution of her plans, of how carefully, anticipating the danger, she watched for the event. Rebekah,

> presuming upon the oracle of God and her husband's simplicity [he writes] dare be his surety for the danger, his counsellor for the carriage of the business, his cook for the diet, yea, dresses both the meat and the man; and now puts words into his mouth, the dish into his hands, the garments upon his back, the goat's hair upon the open parts of his body, and sends him in thus furnished for the blessing, standing no doubt at the door to see how well her device succeeded, and if old Isaac should by any of his senses have discerned the guile, she had soon stept in and undertaken the blame, and urged him with that known will of God concerning Jacob's dominion and Esau's servitude which either age or affection had made him forget.

The offence

Yet in her counter plot Rebekah descends to the level of behaviour she despises in her husband—and she feels so righteous in doing it that she does not see how unrighteous it is! Her very zeal for the Lord seems momentarily to blind her to the issues at stake. If Isaac is shameful, she becomes for a moment shameless. We are meant to be shocked at the sight of her, so dominated by only one consideration that, had even a human life stood in the way of her aim, we doubt if she would have hesitated to sacrifice it. One commentator admits that he finds something almost daemonic in her attitude. 'She sinned grievously', says Calvin, pointing out that she darkened the truth with her lie, provoked her husband's anger, set up an implacable hatred in Esau's heart and risked Jacob's life.

How are we going to find arguments strong enough to justify a mother's deliberately launching her son on such a course of deceit? The story itself in its immediate outcome seems to justify her. But in its final outcome it proves her both wrong and foolish. In the end she is clearly condemned for the risks she took. She brings most bitter consequences both on herself and on her son too. The words with which she urges Jacob on, offering herself to take the consequences if things go astray, sound noble when they are uttered: *Upon me be thy curse, my son* (v. 13 AV), but they too are empty and foolish. Jacob himself has to pay in full for what he does.

Yet even in condemning her, we must admit that we find ourselves excusing her. Was Isaac himself not greatly to blame for Rebekah? In giving him the gift of a wife with such spiritual insight and initiative and willingness for self-sacrifice, did God not mean that he should co-operate and share with her what he had—helping to make her wiser? She, then, by sharing with him, could have made him not only wiser but stronger too. Was it not because he neglected her that, left on her own, she felt impelled to such desperate risks?

9

The Family Crisis—Jacob

GENESIS 27.18–27a

The deed

To gain what he believes is rightfully his, Jacob cunningly steals a march on his brother Esau, dresses in his clothes and impersonates him. He takes advantage of his father's blindness and weakness to deceive him too. All this he does while taking part in a most solemn religious ceremony.

Even the bringing of a sacrifice before the presence of God at an altar was regarded in those days as no holier and no more powerful an action than that in which Jacob engaged with his father. Together they called on the name of the Lord to come into their midst and bless what they were doing.

While playing his part in the action, almost every other phrase Jacob utters is a falsehood (cf. vv. 19, 20, 24). Commentators point out that in his first short, disguised introduction of himself three lies trip over each other (cf. v. 19: I am your *first*-born . . . have *done what you told me* . . . Eat of *my game*). He defends himself against detection by the apt use of pious phraseology. When asked to explain his success in the hunt he is able to soothe with just the correct mixture of handy religious sham: *Because the Lord your God granted me success* (v. 20).

He plays the whole part with the skill of a good actor. The decisive moment of testing comes when Isaac, suddenly suspicious, calls to him: *Come hear, that I may feel you, my son, to know whether you are really my son Esau or not* (v. 21)—and expresses his doubt: *The voice is Jacob's voice.* 'At this point', comments Luther, 'I would have let the dish fall and would have run as though my head were on fire.' But Jacob, cool and practised, does not flinch! If he had trembled— even a little—to show that at least he had in him a few grains of reverence before God! But the only one who trembled on that fateful day in their home was Isaac, and the trembling came later.

As Jacob saw it

If we had been able to interview Jacob we would have understood why he did not tremble. He would have justified his actions, and we would have detected a certain note of holy sincerity in his self-defence. Obviously he was what we call today a 'mixed-up' person. We must try to understand the mixture.

His motives are not discussed in the story, nor are his feelings, except for a hint that, till his mother reassured him, he was afraid of being first found out and then cursed by his father. We have therefore to try to understand him at this point in his life from hints we can gather from elsewhere.

The two great experiences which will dominate the next phase of his life help to explain him as he is at this stage. He has yet to experience his great vision of God and heaven at Bethel (Gen. 28.10-22) and the culminating struggle with God at Peniel (Gen. 32.22-32). At Bethel God was to bring out his innate religious instincts and lead him further into faith in God. At Peniel God was to crush his secularity, his self-reliance. It fits the whole picture well if we assert that his whole early life was dominated by a conflict between these two urges and tendencies.

The tendency to be religious was powerful at first. We cannot with certainty call it 'faith' when it first appeared, but it was there as a strong inner instinct. From his childhood, what Abraham his grandfather was and stood for appealed to him. Above all other things in life, he wanted to be a great man of God and take his place as a true successor to his grandfather. Yet from the start of his life there was also in him something tough, cunning, evasive, pushing and competitive. We remember that the name 'Jacob' means 'supplanter'. At the time of this incident the two instincts are still struggling within him on almost equal terms. No priority has become established. He is simply a confused individual who doesn't quite know in which direction he wants to go.

However, when his mother suddenly challenges him and he realizes that the future of the blessing and the promise of Abraham are at stake, then in all sincerity he enlists every natural talent he has, all his skill and cunning too, in the service of the Lord. The inner entanglement of his life is such that he cannot separate one aspect from another.

As God saw it

Throughout the incident no aspect of Jacob's behaviour is criticized either by the writer or by his mother or father, or by God. Indeed God seems to approve of what he does, for he is allowed to succeed. People with Jacob's tendency to self-reliance in the service of God are only too prone to see success as a sign of God's approval of their action.

Yet, without any doubt, there were aspects of what Jacob did on that night which God, even in showing mercy to Jacob, caused to have the most painful outcome. And at the same time he made sure that Jacob and those who tried to follow in his steps would know that in this case B followed A—i.e. that the evil deed brought about the painful consequences.

We can trace the matter through as we read the history. Jacob is forced to flee from home. In his exile he is brought under the power of a villain no less cunning and ruthless in the pursuit of his aims than he himself has been. He is tricked by this man exactly as he himself has tricked his brother (Gen. 29). When he later tries to escape from his clutches, he is reduced to such a state of humiliation that only God, by a miracle, saves him from a kind of perpetual slavery (Gen. 31). And then before he is forced again to face his cheated brother, he has to settle with God face to face as to which aspect of his nature is going to have full control (Gen. 32). As N. Sarna puts it, 'An explicit denunciation [of Jacob's lapse] could hardly have been more effective or more scathing than this unhappy biography.'

Jacob has to learn that God, for the sake of the honour of his name and the fulfilment of his loving purpose for this world, expects a far higher standard from people who profess to be his witnesses than from any others. If Jacob is so determined to serve God—so be it. God will accept him. But let him learn by experience as well as by words and commandments what it means to follow in the footsteps of Abraham. What kind of a reputation would God have had within the developing life of Jacob's growing family, if he had not taught him in this way about his holiness? What kind of a God would they grow up to tell the world he was?

What God must have hated most in the affair of the blessing was the pretence which Jacob introduced into such a solemn act of worship. The commandment not to 'take the name of the Lord in vain' has priority in the decalogue, even over that forbidding murder. Time and again in Old Testament days it was noted with dread that when people approached the holy place, or handled the holy things of God, insincerely, they could be visited suddenly with devastating punishment—as King Uzziah for example was immediately struck with leprosy (2 Chron. 26.18 ff.). Time and again the prophets preached that God hated, above all other things, to have people drawing near to him with their lips when their heart was far from him (Isa. 29.13). Jacob was spared immediate condemnation because his heart to some extent was seeking God. But he had to be taught his lesson.

As we ourselves can see it

Some aspects of this story are lit up for us by church history itself. It is, after all, the story of a man carried away into deceit and theft by a zeal for God that was not informed or controlled by true understanding of knowledge. We can think, of course, of the Pharisees and of the Jews in their rejection of Christ: 'They have a zeal for God,' said Paul, 'but it is not enlightened' (Rom. 10.2). We can also think of the official 'inquisitions' set up at times by churches both Roman and Protestant, in which a partially ignorant establishment, inspired only by blind zeal for what had been defined as orthodoxy, yet without a true understanding of the nature and feeling of God himself, in the name of God tried to deprive others of their rights and standing before him.

Sometimes today we ourselves may be tempted to play a part like Jacob's. Certainly we will often find him around us. Many people—especially the young—are showing an unusual interest in what is religious or 'transcendental', claiming to have had spiritual experiences of great variety. The desire to have a further blessing from God, to explore and share such experiences with others, can become a passion so dominant that all restraints and all other considerations are lost sight of.

Where we find such enthusiasts we will always, too, find someone like Rebekah, though often not so sincere as she or Jacob—a leader or promoter with a plan and a purpose, ready to encourage and recruit. We well know what can happen. The mature knowledge of who God is, of what he really wants in life, may be lacking. The ability for self-criticism that comes from a truer experience of the working of the human mind and heart before God may be lacking. The knowledge of what life is really all about is lacking—but a zeal is there to the full! That is why we have the sects, the deviant cults, or the strange new religions, in which

63

devotees can be led in the name of supposed truth into all kinds of foolish and hurtful ways.

Sometimes we justify our bold new departures from love, righteousness and our best traditions by the name of Jesus who died on the cross. We are meant to notice in this story that if Jacob had been left to himself he would have been too afraid of being cursed to have gone ahead. He was actually emboldened to proceed by the solemn oath of his mother: 'Upon me be your curse, my son' (27.13). She would bear what he might deserve!

Our Lord himself is the only one who ever had a right to say such a thing as Rebekah said. He took the curse of all our sins, actual and possible—of all our sacrilege and insincerity and hypocrisy. How dreadful a thing it is that sometimes, today, his very love in doing this for us should embolden us to attitudes and approaches that are unworthy.

10

The Family Crisis—God!

GENESIS 27.27b-33

Intervention and follow-up

A miracle is needed, and it must happen soon, if the life of this family is to be healed.

The story from now on, for at least the next six chapters, is of this miraculous work of God. It takes the form of one sudden, decisive intervention, followed by a long process of breaking up, of healthy change and new development, itself punctuated by further dramatic, divine interventions. For

there is much work to do. In healing these family affairs
God must first get Isaac back to the place where Abraham
was. He has to take this cunning and far-too-daring man,
Jacob, firmly into his hands. He has to settle things between
the brothers. He has to bring Rebekah, too, to her senses.
He has to deal personally with Esau in a way that will be
recognized as right.

Each one of these people is treated differently. Esau, from
his own entirely worldly point of view, is treated most
leniently of all. Though he momentarily feels the temporary
loss of face, in the end he loses only what he does not value.
His health, his wives are left untouched, and his property is
actually increased. It is the others, who will have to become
examples to the world, who come under the more severe
treatment. Isaac, it is to be noted, is treated in a much
gentler way than Rebekah or Jacob. After all, though he has
certainly just gone through a period that was for him
disgraceful, God can remember how, time and again, and
especially on Mount Moriah (Gen. 22), he has shown that
the deepest desire of his life has been for God and his will.
It does not take so much to bring him back to where he has
once been.

God's presence!

The intervention of God begins at the very moment when
Jacob, setting his seal to the whole farcical intrigue, stoops
to kiss his father and to let him smell Esau's garments. Isaac
does not understand, at that moment, the significance of
what has happened, but he knows himself beyond all doubt
seized by a sudden inspiration, speaking under the power
and presence of God himself: and he blessed him and said

*See, the smell of my son, is as the smell of a field which the
Lord has blessed! May God give you the dew of heaven, and
of the fatness of the earth, and plenty of grain and wine. Let*

65

peoples serve you, and nations bow down to you. Be lord over your brothers, and may your mother's sons bow down to you. Cursed be everyone who curses you, and blessed be everyone who blesses you! (vv. 27b-29).

It was a memorable ecstatic experience, comparable to that which came to Melchizedek, for example, when he blessed Abraham after his victory over the five kings (Gen. 14.19; cf. *Abraham*, pp. 36-8), or to Balaam when, in spite of his attempt to curse Israel, God took over his tongue and he blessed them (Num. 24.15). The words which came to Isaac gripped both speaker and hearer. They poured out of him, carrying power, truth and a healthy influence to the man before him (cf. v. 33!). Surely it meant a great destiny for the son for whose sake such an inspiration had been given!

Rebekah (she must have been eavesdropping!) felt at that moment that God had crowned her plan with success and had answered her prayers. Jacob may not have appreciated fully what had taken place, but at least he thought he had it all fixed up at last! So it began—the healing of this family—charismatically, like a New Testament experience of being 'filled with the Holy Spirit'.

God's freedom

Is God acting wrongly here? We deliberately repeat what we have already said: Any fair examination of the minds and attitude of these three people before God must lead to the conclusion that what each first needed was not blessing but correction—a re-orientation of life, moral uplift, more concern for people other than themselves. And yet God ignored their immediate needs and began by pouring out his blessing on them—which made them feel good and safe.

Can our interpretation of the incident be wrong? Does it not seem to contradict what the Bible says elsewhere about

God's holiness? For it seems to bring him down with great and free blessing into the heart of human disobedience and insincerity. It seems to make his grace cheap. It can suggest that even the Holy Supper of our Lord can come in power to 'unworthy' people without their already showing signs of repentance.

Though we have to admit the force of such objections we still believe our interpretation of this incident to be the only one possible. Therefore we have to acknowledge, and even be glad, that sometimes, before God brings people under strict discipline and changes them in any radical way, he first makes them certain of his favour in such an exciting manner. Of course Isaac will soon be trembling, Rebekah will soon be counting the cost of what she has done, Jacob will soon find himself submitting to the heavy hand laid on him. But for the moment it is real joy.

To find any other incident quite like this in the Bible we have to turn to the New Testament to meet Jesus eating and drinking with publicans and sinners. Can we not justifiably see Isaac and Rebekah and Jacob there? We doubt if many of those people around Jesus were committed to follow him. Yet some of them had experienced a moment or two of great emotion as they heard him speaking to them about God and themselves. It was no doubt later, as they followed him, that they came to the place of trembling and to the beginning of a painful process of recovery.

Some of us tend to react too quickly and unfavourably against those who seek today to give room in the Church to such enthusiastic and exciting new beginnings—against, for example, the evangelist who seeks signs of God's renewing in 'conversions' and other definitely felt experiences of joy. We tend to be especially critical when we see no immediate moral points appearing, and no attempt even in the preaching to awaken social conscience as the soul is awakened.

Is not a story like this in the Bible to save us from becoming too dogmatic about the order God should take in

67

doing his work? Can we not trust him if he cares to deal with people today in the same very dangerous way? In the history of the Church, for many who later became steady and hard-working Christians in their day, the new life began simply as with Wesley—with 'a heart strangely warmed'!

Let us be prepared to allow God his full freedom to come into the midst, when and how he wills. I remember a group of students during the racial tension in the southern United States, who sincerely felt that there could be no grace of God working in those Churches which at that time supported segregation and refused to admit blacks to their communion. Some time before they discussed the matter with me, I had celebrated the Lord's Supper in an exclusive little church at the heart of one of these white communities. When I suggested to the group that that was a valid sacrament, and that Christ had been present really to give himself even to those racists who still had some faith in him, I met no support—only the suspicion that I too was tainted with racism.

The reawakening of Isaac

Esau returns from his hunting happy and confident. He has been successful and he is already feeling blessed: *Let my father arise, and eat of his son's game, that you may bless me* (v. 31).

For Isaac, the joyful fervency of his inspired moment is replaced first by shock, then by horror and confusion: *Who are you?* and *Who was it then that hunted game and brought it to me, and I ate it all before you came, and I have blessed him?* (v. 33).

As he says it he *trembles violently* (v. 33). He does not need to be told who it is. He now knows. Isaac, blind Isaac, is shocked. And he realizes that God has seen it all. He knows that even during his insane folly all his moves have been open before God. His heart has been read. His intentions have been probed. Yet all the time, graciously and with unerring wisdom and power, he has been controlled and used by the same God, the holy and faithful friend of his father, who has refused to turn away his face from him in disgust and shame.

He confesses himself confused and stupid as he trembles: *I have blessed him?* (v. 33)—it is an admission that he has been deceived, not by Jacob but by God. What a fool he has been, trying to play his game cleverly before God!

He surrenders totally to God as he confesses. Now he wills wholly to have what God has willed. He submits to the overruling. He will not try to deny the certainty of that great and inspired moment when God took his tongue and inspired him to utter the benediction. God placed Jacob there instead of Esau. God forced him out of his error into the right way. *I have blessed him?—yes, and he shall be blessed* (v. 33).

We are given only two more glimpses of Isaac after this incident closes. In the one we see him now open to discussion with Rebekah about the family. In the other we see him repeating his blessing of Jacob. Now, no longer a fool thinking he can hide, he will live like a friend in the open before the eyes of God.

O Lord, thou hast searched me and known me!

The 139th Psalm was written under the excitement of a great discovery the psalmist had just made about God, himself and life. It seems to have come to him suddenly. He has become aware of how from the beginning of his days and at every stage of his past life all his thoughts and deeds, even all the tendencies of his mind and heart, have been like an open book before God. He had tried, as subtly as he could, to hide things in himself and had hoped they would be hidden, but even when he had wanted the dark to cover him the darkness had been as light to God:

> O Lord, thou hast searched me and known me!
> Thou knowest when I sit down and when I rise
>   up;
> Thou discernest my thoughts from afar.
> Thou searchest out my path and my lying down,
> And art acquainted with all my ways (Ps. 139.1-3).

We do not know how the psalmist was led to make his discovery. But his reaction when he has made it is worth comparing with Isaac's. The psalmist too trembles as the patriarch did—and the thought occurs of going from God's presence even to Sheol, the place of the dead! But he realizes that God is too tenacious, too strong for him ever to hope to escape, and too loving not to be there now, as he has always been. Indeed he realizes that in God's searching presence there is only one way now to live (and indeed to live for ever). He wants simply to remain always thus, open before God, to live there from day to day finding his sole comfort and hope in the fact that God always thinks and plans for him. Never may it become otherwise!

> Search me, O God, and know my heart!
> Try me and know my thoughts!
> And see if there be any wicked way in me,
> and lead me in the way everlasting! (Ps. 139.23-4).

It is agreed by all discerning commentators that this Psalm is one of the greatest utterances of true personal piety in the Bible. In it, the faith and devotion of Abraham and his successors come to their finest expression before the coming of Christ. Yet, though it took so many centuries to attain such full expression in the Psalm, the heart of it is there already in the trembling discovery and submission of Isaac in God's presence.

It is in the presence of Christ that we too make this discovery today—more simply, more fully, even more searchingly than either Isaac or the psalmist. It is in the presence of Christ that we too discover the answer to the question of eternity: whether we *want* to be searched and known.

A story of late tradition in the New Testament tells how a woman was caught in the act of committing adultery. The penalty was to be death by stoning. Before they administered the sentence, her accusers took her to Jesus, pointed to her and named her sin. They wanted to know whether he was ready to uphold the law of Moses which prescribed such a death. But Jesus took time, was silent, and wrote something in the sand—possibly words reminding them of what he had said about adultery within the human heart. A miraculous change took place in the whole atmosphere. The men began to feel uncomfortable. Jesus challenged whoever was without sin to begin the stoning. Her accusers, feeling themselves exposed, all left her alone with the Lord.

To leave his presence when it became searching was their condemnation. They hated the light but she alone, exposed too, stayed on in his presence. She was content to remain in the light. No wonder he did not condemn her! (Cf. John 8.1 ff. margin.)

11

The Family Crisis—Esau

GENESIS 27.34-28.9

'He found no way open for second thoughts'

The story is now about Esau. Like Isaac, he finds himself exposed. If he too had been willing openly to face the pressure of God's near presence and the truth which God was bringing into the situation during that moment at his father's bedside, then there could have been for him also, as for all the others, the beginning of a renewal. Of him, too, was now required acceptance of God's declared will about the 'blessing'. If he had assented, then a place of honour and service could have been found for him within the unity of the family of God.

His deep emotion, at the moment, makes our heart want to go out to him. There is, it seems, as much pathos in his *great and bitter cry* (v. 34: *Bless me, even me also, O my father!*) as in David's lament over the death of his beloved Absalom: 'O my son Absalom, Absalom, my son, my son!' (2 Sam. 19.4). Surely, we feel, there must be seeds of real goodness in his hurt over what he has lost, in the passion with which he seems to want it restored, and in the trust and love with which he now clings to his father!

The New Testament writer who discusses this incident warns us against such a superficial judgement. Esau, at this very moment, he affirms, reveals himself again as he did when he sold his birthright. He was then, now and always an 'immoral and irreligious' man (Heb. 12.16). 'For you know that afterwards, when he desired to inherit the blessing, he was rejected, for he found no chance to repent, though he sought it with tears' (Heb. 12.17). Esau, he

72

affirms, was rejected by God at this moment, not because God had predetermined to reject him but because of his reaction to what God was doing there and then.

When Esau returned from his hunting that day, he confronted an entirely new situation in his home life. God had come to be present, to redirect and renew everyone and everything within the family circle. Esau, openly and with firm determination, put himself out of the way into which God was now moving affairs. He refused to fit into the new conditions of life with God. He willed to have things back where they were. He had always considered himself as set up by God to be dignified as the worthy successor of Abraham. So firm was he in his determination that it should be so, that he would not, and could not, submit to what had taken place. Two of our modern translations of the phrase, 'he found no chance to repent', are revealing: 'he was unable to elicit a change of heart', says one (JB); 'he found no way open for second thoughts', says another (NEB).

The sham

Sorrow, often to the point of tears, can sometimes accompany a true repentance which has its deeper roots in a change of mind and will. When we discover the sorrow our life has caused to God and the damage we have done to others, are we not bound to give expression to contrition of heart?

Esau throws himself into all the emotions that normally go with repentance. He weeps with deep sorrow. But his weeping arises from his resentment at being personally and completely frustrated. He is not weeping towards God or before God. He is not praying to God, but to his earthly father alone: *O my father* (v. 34) . . . *my father . . . father!* (v. 38). This is why the New Testament writer calls him 'irreligious' (Heb. 12.16; cf. also NEB 'worldly-minded', NIV 'godless'). His 'repentance' is described by Luther as 'gallows repentance'—that of one who is sorry, not because

73

he has offended God, but because of where his offence has brought him.

We are meant to notice that Esau, whose professed desire to have the genuine thing had been superficial, is anxious to make up the loss on the superficial level. Let his father, then, extract from God what is next best, and at least he will feel comforted. So he now seeks some kind of a 'blessing'— any kind will do!—as a substitute for the genuine thing. Isaac does his best. He no doubt prays and receives inspiration. He gives what God allows him to give. But the Spirit will not allow him to be fulsome and flattering—as we Christians often are to unbelievers about their destiny. It is a moment in which truth must be spoken, even in love. Esau will certainly succeed in the life he has learned to love most, the life of the hunter in the wilds: *Behold, away from the fatness of the earth shall your dwelling be, and away from the dew of heaven from on high. By your sword you shall live, and you shall serve your brother; but when you break loose you shall break his yoke from your neck.* (vv. 39–40). But there is no mention of life, or blessing, with God.

The hatred

The New Testament writer whose views we have been discussing uses the case of Esau as a warning to us to 'see to it . . . that no "root of bitterness" spring up and cause trouble' (Heb. 12.15).

Esau illustrates the trouble that such a 'root of bitterness' can cause. He feels it within him as soon as he discovers his loss. His first cry of anguish expresses the feeling of it: 'an exceedingly great and bitter cry' (v. 34). His choice is clear. He can surrender either to God or to this bitterness. He deliberately chooses the way of bitterness: *Now Esau hated Jacob because of the blessing with which his father had blessed him, and Esau said to himself, 'The days of mourning for my father are approaching; then I will kill my brother Jacob'*

(v. 41). Because he will not change in face of God, he has to harden himself with spite in face of God. He will wait! Nothing will be done in the moment of excusable passion. Everything will be allowed to cool and thus become deliberate. It will be carefully planned and well done.

It is not just personal hatred or envy that is the driving motive. When such hatred cools, often the urge to kill can die away. The hatred that possesses Esau, however, is of the kind that made Cain kill Abel. Cain was angry first, not at his brother but at God himself. Then he transferred his hatred to his brother, on whom God had bestowed favour. Cain's crime was a blow at God and his favourite chosen for his work. This is the hatred that possesses Esau. It is the eternal hatred of the serpent for God and his human race. When it cools down from its occasional heights of passion, it remains no less strong in the will and mind than it has been in the emotion. It is there directing behaviour, aiming criticism and persecution. It will seek to crush Christian piety and evangelical faith. Whatever God really blesses will incur its mad opposition. It is the kind of hatred that broke out all round Jesus when he came, and which drove men to crucify him—most of them also in an act of cool, calculated spite because they would not have any other rule than that of themselves.

The awakening of Rebekah

When Rebekah hears of the vow of Esau to kill Jacob, she knows that she too is being faced by a word of God: this is what she herself has brought about by her folly! Her conscience gives her no relief. We are not told of her trembling or of her sorrow. They must have been there, accompanying her repentance—and no doubt the tears kept coming, later, many times, and never grew less when they came.

To repent, however, is not merely to weep but to act and,

if need be, to plan. In repentance we have to contrive as far as we ourselves can to put things right. Rebekah does all this. It is to her honour that she acts out of love for Esau (v. 45), whom she tries to save from the anger she has provoked. But she must also save Jacob. She therefore rapidly decides that what is good for both men is God's will, and she accepts it thankfully. She puts on an astonishingly brave face to see the matter through.

The home situation is better than before. She can now go to Isaac and talk sensibly with him about the problem: in case Jacob is now tempted like Esau to make an impossible marriage, why not send him away to Paddan-aram to find a wife among the daughters of Laban her brother? It is to her credit that she withholds the true reason for her suggestion. She wants, out of love, to spare the old man the sorrow she deserves to bear herself. Did she not vow to take all the curse of her son's behaviour on herself? She has already borne much of it in the most painful moment when she had to tell Jacob the truth and urge him to flee from her and his brother (vv. 43-5).

The suffering she has to undergo as a result of what has happened is heavier than Isaac's. Professedly and outwardly she comforts herself with the hope that Esau's anger will soon pass, and she will see Jacob again, but it is likely that in her heart she knows it will be a long and bitter exile for him and for her, and she gradually comes to realize that she may never see him again.

Yet even under this burden there is an admirable dignity about her. As if God is setting his seal of approval on the greatness of her faith, he allows her in complete freedom to pass this sentence of death upon herself. She is not abruptly taken to task, verbally condemned, constrained to accept some punishment. God, for her sake, works it all gently and reasonably. Again, he has taken her up on the vow she made to Jacob—to take the curse willingly on herself. This is the kind of woman God is dealing with. Even in allowing her to reap something of what she has sown, he will respect her freedom and let her bear what comes as an offering now willingly given in the service of his righteousness and his name.

A last lingering look

Before the writer passes on to discuss what happened to Jacob—for we are now to spend many years with him—he allows us to see what Esau did when he heard his father forbidding Jacob to take a wife from the heathen women around him and dismissing him to Paddan-aram to find the right woman. *So when Esau saw that the Canaanite women did not please Isaac his father, Esau went to Ishmael and took to wife, besides the wives he had, Mahalath the daughter of Ishmael, Abraham's son* (vv. 8-9).

We can of course interpret this act as an illustration of the love of the superficial that is so characteristic of anything Esau does which has any religious significance—as if such a pathetic gesture could compensate for his previous willful marriages. But this fresh incident may be told in order to suggest something more. Is Esau now wakening up to see how foolish he had been to take the Hittite women as wives? Moreover, his desire to please his father is emphasized (Gen. 28.8), and we now look back and notice that the reason he gave for not killing Jacob immediately was a professed reluctance to hurt his father so long as he was alive (Gen. 27.41).

Is the writer, then, trying to suggest to us that there may still be something good in this man—better than we had thought at the time when he made his vow to kill his brother? If so, it is a very small and very frail root of something beginning to try to grow in strange soil! And by the time we see Esau again, he is still possessed by his desire for vengeance.

But the hint has been dropped to us to keep us from

finally deciding too dogmatically about Esau. We have to remember that even Cain one day came to despair, and God then set on him a mark of hope (Gen. 4.15). The writers of the Bible do not want us to close the books too quickly in order to start counting the number of the damned. Indeed, they want to encourage us, today and always, to look at what is worthwhile laying hold of in our hope, and worthwhile praying for.

So we have a lingering look at Esau before he leaves us for a long time. It reminds us of the lingering and prayerful look at another 'hopeless' case. Of the rich young ruler who 'went away sorrowful', we are told that 'Jesus looking upon him loved him' (Mark 10.21), and commenting on his case later he said: 'What is impossible with men, is possible with God' (Luke 18.27 NEB).

In face of people who appear at first to be committed to evil, we are encouraged to go on praying. We are told not to quarrel with the person who, it seems, cannot repent because he has shut his mind, but to try to correct him with gentleness, for 'God may perhaps grant that they will repent and come to know the truth' (2 Tim. 2.25; cf. also 1 Tim. 2.4). Perhaps!—this word is worth holding on to, even in the case of Esau. He was still Rebekah's boy. She loved him. She was praying.

12

Bethel—I: The Vision

GENESIS 28.10-13

A new backdrop for life and for God

The trickery to which Jacob descended in his efforts to obtain both the 'birthright' and the 'blessing' shows how unfitted he was to have them. But it also indicates his belief that he was the one called by God to succeed Abraham and Isaac in leading his family on towards the great things God had promised to do through it.

He knew what was implied in fulfilling the call. He must become a man of God. No other interpretation will do justice to the whole account we have of Jacob except one which assumes that from the very beginning of his life, and steadily throughout it, he wanted above everything else the experience, the knowledge, the dedication implied in seeking the privilege. He was a man who wanted God.

Yet though the desire was there, the fulfilment almost completely eluded him. Obviously he did not know the kind of God his fathers had learned to trust in and worship. Moreover, even though as a shepherd he must have met some of the difficulties and dangers of life in the open, the impression we are given of him at this stage is that what most mattered to him in life was contained within a very small circumference. His religion was geared only to family history and family affairs. His life was lived among the tents, between the kitchen, the table and father's bedside. His two great adventures had been cheating Esau over the birthright and supplanting him at the blessing. In his success in these affairs he must have felt that somehow God helped him. But even a quite small god, working on a small scale with quite questionable moral attributes, would have been adequate to explain what had happened. Jacob, with all the basic desire of his heart, crying out for the living God, was as mixed up in his theology as we have already suggested him to be in his psychology (see p. 60).

Sometimes a play in a theatre begins with a few actors on a narrow front strip of the stage, hedged thickly at the back by a plain confining curtain. As the action proceeds, the confining backdrop is lifted and the huge stage is seen, with new dimensions and perspectives opened out to the eye by a more distant and wider back screen. Then in the bigger context the greater issues begin to be unfolded.

Quite suddenly it happens in this way with Jacob that night at Bethel. He is on the first leg of his journey to Paddan-aram. He arrives tired and lonely. No doubt when he sees the bleakness of the spot—*the stones of the place* (v. 11)—he is tempted to give way to gloom and to ask what, really, the future can hold for him. It happens to him as it was to happen centuries later to John in similar circumstances on a rocky prison island: 'I looked, and lo, in heaven an open door!' (Rev. 4.1).

We are told by Old Testament scholars that the imagery which Jacob saw in his dream comes from what he knew, or could picture, of the structure of the Mesopotamian and Babylonian temples of his day. These had high temple towers in which the god was supposed to dwell. They had also ground-level temples where the god was believed, on occasion, to appear. In between the heavenly tower and the earthly gate there was usually a long ramp (the 'ladder' in the vision). The Babylonians thought that this ramp linked heaven and earth. The fact that some of the contents of the dream could have had such origins need not prevent God from using them effectively to teach Jacob what no true Babylonian could ever have begun to understand.

Though the vision is of such short duration, and though he hears only one speech, Jacob is helped by God to see that

GENESIS 28.10-13

the world in which he now has to live has a far more mysterious background and far greater dimensions and possibilities than he has ever before imagined. He is led to understand that the concerns to which he must now open his mind in thinking about the God of his fathers are far bigger and more urgent than he has ever tried honestly to face. He observes at the same time that his family's God, who has spoken to him, is strong enough and exalted enough to cope with such a universe and all its affairs.

He sees another realm—a kingdom!—besides the one in which he has travelled and eaten and slept. He sees creatures and powers that belong to the other realm rather than to this. He sees in it the place of God himself, the ruler and creator of this world. He sees that there is a way or a ladder from one world to another, and traffic going on between.

The vision teaches him about the power and the near presence of the God who loves him. 'God Almighty appeared to me' (Gen. 48.3), he will say later, thinking about the place of this vision. Up till now he has certainly thought of God as intimately involved in his own family's little history, and in the history of the earth. But here is God above all history, with bigger plans and infinitely greater resources at his disposal than Jacob has ever dreamed of. *This* is the God who appears 'to *me*'—the God who still loves his Jacob, and speaks to him!

From Jacob to Jesus

We call Jacob's vision a theophany—a visual appearance in which God presents himself in such a way that people can say they have 'seen' him. Abraham saw such theophanies (Gen. 12.7, 15.1, 17.1) and they happened at other times in Israel's history (e.g. Exod. 19.16 ff., 24.11).

Some writers think that such theophanies or appearings of God were expected to take place at certain points in the liturgy of worship and celebration where people gathered to participate in the great feasts at the temple. There are prayers in the Psalms for God to come and meet his people, to 'make his face shine' and to appear to them with the light of his countenance so that they could 'see' him (e.g. Pss. 4.6; 17.15; 67.1; Num. 6.26). It is suggested that these prayers reflect the fact that ordinary people encountered God there in some way through vision as well as through word. We know that Isaiah had a vision something like that of Jacob when he was, no doubt, at worship in the temple (Isa. 6.1 ff.).

Though such visions may have been experienced frequently by ordinary people, we have only a few detailed descriptions of them. We have this one from the history of Jacob, we have another from Moses (Exod. 34.6ff.); we have those of Isaiah and of Ezekiel (Ezek. 1.4 ff.). The accounts of what took place in these visions have had a very great influence in helping other people to pray better and to think about God.

We must admit that the theophany given to Moses personally by God was much more powerful and striking than that given to Jacob. And those given to Isaiah and Ezekiel were much more elaborate and developed. Yet it may be said that the Bethel story has nearly always remained one of the favourite and one of the most influential stories of the whole Bible. It is retold again and again. It has never failed to enrich the traditions by which Jacob's successors have been helped to understand God himself, and the background of life in this world into which he has put us. God had in mind many more than just one man in what was shown and said that night at Bethel.

There was, therefore, much more in Jacob's vision than Jacob himself grasped at the time he saw it. When God reveals things to any of us through the Bible he always puts much more into what he gives us than we can grasp at that moment. He allows our minds always to be making progress

82

towards what is already there in the Word. Our vision is bigger than our thought can comprehend.

It is Jesus who finally shows us what God is really trying to say to us in Jacob's vision, and it is his use of it which makes it important for us to think seriously about its meaning. Referring to the Bethel incident, he said to one of his disciples (who had no doubt been thinking about it!), 'Truly, truly, I say to you, you will see the heaven opened, and the angels of God ascending and descending upon the Son of man' (John 1.1). Now that Jesus is here, we are to be able to understand what happened there.

In many of his parables, Jesus spoke of the 'Kingdom of God' or 'the Kingdom of heaven'. He described it as a realm of glory and wealth worth finding above all other treasures (Matt. 13.44-15)—of feasting, joy and fellowship with God (Luke 14.15-24; Matt. 8.11). He spoke of its closeness to earth (Luke 17.20), of how easy it was for believing and repentant individuals to enter it, and of the welcome we would receive when we entered (Luke 15.22-4). He spoke of the traffic between this Kingdom and the present world (Matt. 26.53; John 10.9, 5.24), the miraculous and transforming influence that its powerful and near presence could have on the diseases people suffered and on their daily lives (Luke 11.20). He spoke of how the pressure it exerted on public affairs was going to determine the ultimate course of this world's history (Matt. 13.24 ff.).

When Jesus spoke of all this and tried to demonstrate it, he was describing and indeed pointing to something which corresponds to what Jacob saw in his vision. Of course the early vision was not nearly so elaborate, not so down-to-earth, not so influential in the affairs of the world. The ladder of access was not yet so firmly built into the earth, and it was angels rather than sinners who were ascending and descending. But it was nevertheless this kingdom which Jesus described. He himself brought it near (Matt. 3.2).

Jesus, moreover, expected us to be able to say we have

seen it (John 3.3), and to know that we have entered it (John 3.5, 5.24). He asked us also, in our thinking about God, to try to see him, as Jacob did, in his relationship with this 'other' realm as well as within our present world. When you pray, say, 'Our Father who art in heaven' (Matt. 6.9). He is the 'Father', with family feeling, involved closely with us in our joys and troubles, compassionate and seeking fellowship. He is 'in heaven'—serene in this compassionate love, always there, yet always above us, unaffected by our trouble in his power to save and help, to be trusted whatever the earthly difficulty. Though he seeks a kingdom here, he has a much better one elsewhere—which he wills to share with us too!

Life today and the Kingdom of God

It must be admitted that some of us today in our ideas of God and our dealings with him tend to revert to where Jacob was in his raw youth. We confine God to our piety, and domesticate him. The world in which we try to live with him, the affairs in which we instinctively turn to him, and to which we refer him, our thoughts of what he wants to do for us, are often only personal and sometimes petty. He is not much more to us than a psychological counsellor, family doctor and mother's help in one small package.

Though he is kind enough to bear with us, and care for us, even though we belittle him in our thoughts in such a way, he wants us to grow up! Some of us try. We manage to get our ideas of God above the individual and domestic level. We learn to refer him to our politics, and our politics to him. We relate him to our social conditions. We show the place he must be given in the counsels of all nations. Our faith sees him actively at work on the largest scale of human history. We see him in the stars and in the microscope. We see him involved in the whole course of the evolution of the world and of life.

Yet there is a quite other dimension into which we have

to move in order to see both God and life properly: the world invisible, the world to come, of which Jacob had his glimpse. This world was there before ours began and will continue to be there hereafter.

Far too many of us do not try to reach it even in thought. Our minds are too much dominated by 'enlightenment' and 'science', and we are far too afraid of becoming trapped in what we think is outmoded biblical mythology for us ever to enter the Kingdom of heaven! Therefore we pay the price. Our world remains too small and God too remains small. We may call the universe of which we have managed to conceive vast, infinite, even 'eternal'—but we can still measure it in terms of billions of billions and we can hope that it will all be finally computed. It is indeed vast, but it is also so small that for us there is no room left in it for miracle here and now, for the transcendent, for the New Creation, the greater and much more glorious universe which is to come!

Our stage-front is too cramped. We must allow God to lift the confining backdrop of our own making! For there behind it the heavens are opened. By his grace we can be brought to see the great cloud of those whose witness is meant to inspire us to run the race set before us (Heb. 12.1); and the judge of all the earth enthroned, to whose tribunal the path of each one of us unerringly leads (Rev. 20.11 ff.): the 'King in his beauty' in the land which 'stretches afar' (Isa. 33.17) where life is without pain, sorrow, death, or any restriction (Rev. 21.4).

We can help our comprehension by the submission and discipline of our mind before the Word of God where it is shown to us. But we also need to be helped to see, by the Spirit who opens the eyes and fulfils the promise of Jesus that all around him people would be given the power to 'see' (Matt. 13.16); and there is one place where it is certainly good that we should begin to look. 'How awesome is this place', Jacob said (Gen. 28.16), the 'gate of heaven'! For him it was Bethel—dark, bleak, stony! For us it is the cross.

> O safe and happy shelter!
> O refuge tried and sweet!
> O trysting-place where heaven's love
> And heaven's justice meet!
> As to the exiled patriarch
> That wondrous dream was given,
> So seems my Saviour's Cross to me
> A ladder up to heaven.
> *(Elizabeth C. Clephane, d. 1869)*

13

Bethel—II: The Word

GENESIS 28.13–22

The living voice

The God of the Bible is one who concentrates more on what he can achieve by speaking than on what he can convey through visual imagery (cf. Deut. 4.12). He desires, in the first place, that people should believe by hearing his voice (cf. Deut. 6.4). Visions and visible signs, when added, are usually to confirm and illustrate what he is saying in his Word. Therefore the voice, at Bethel, and what the voice says, matter to Jacob even more than the vision. It is the voice which takes Jacob directly to the heart of what God wants to give him and seeks to have from him. The vision is its background.

Jacob knows it is the living voice of God himself—the same voice that came to Abraham, that greatest of men! His own father, too, in his day has heard it. But never before has Jacob. He has seen evidence of its having been spoken. He has heard his father witnessing to it. In his most recent experience at home, when his father was seized by the Spirit to bless him, he has felt very near to something like it.

Now the voice comes addressed to himself, as a person called, as it were, by his name; and he hears God, not man. It comes in the same way as we sometimes hope and pray it may come to us when the Word of God is preached in our church, and we listen. Surely this hearing by Jacob gives us the clue as to why we go to listen there today! Did he hear anything different, anything less or more wonderful than we too can expect to hear in our pew?

When the voice comes, he knows himself called, comforted, and challenged as he has not been before—invited into a close and warm relationship, but at the same time constrained to surrender and service. But he knows he is also enabled to serve, for the voice itself brings some measure of God's own vitality—even something of himself!—into Jacob's life. It stirs up things within him at a deeper level than other people have ever done.

Liturgy and life

Something else is happening. What God speaks, he has spoken before, again and again. Jacob's own father has repeated it personally to him twice before, and very solemnly. It begins exactly as if it were printed in a prayer book for daily recitation: it sounds, after so much usage and development, beautiful and rhythmical:

I am the Lord, the God of Abraham your father and the God

87

of Isaac; the land on which you lie I will give to your
descendants; and your descendants shall be like the dust of the
earth, and you shall spread abroad to the west and to the east
and to the north and to the south; and by you and your
descendants will all the families of the earth bless themselves
(vv. 13–14).

Perhaps Jacob has always loved hearing the words of these
promises even when they were simply being repeated on
human lips. He likes the rhythm of the language, the poetic
forms into which the promises were sometimes put. But it
has all been mere liturgy and hearsay. Now the liturgy and
hearsay have become reality. The word spoken *about* God
has become the word *of* God. And at the heart of it he hears
it say, 'I love you!'

Much of what God speaks to us today in our worship and
much of what we speak to him in response is in such
'liturgical' form. It has been spoken in this way and in these
very forms for centuries. We have to confess that sometimes
we have used such forms and hymns in worship without any
feeling that we could put ourselves into the acts of worship
into which they were supposed to lead us. They did not
inwardly and in reality seem to lead us to God as they
outwardly professed to do. When we felt satisfaction, it was
in the pleasure we took in the traditional beauty of the forms
and even of the accompanying music rather than in anything
we could call real experience of God. Therefore there has
often been a call for change—to new forms, more relevant
and alive, because they use the emphases of more modern
thought and more up-to-date language.

However much we may yearn for worship in contemporary
style and idiom, let us never forget that liturgy can only
come alive, not through our skill in coining new and fitting
devotional phrases but through the Spirit of God coming to
take and inspire what is being used as an offering in God's
service. Here is a hint that it will not be in vain for us to seek

to meet him and to make an offering to him in well-trodden paths.

When the liturgy begins to take life, it spills out into a personal message in which Jacob finds that his most urgent needs of the moment are being met by one who understands exactly where he has come from and where he is going. His sin and folly have cut him off from his family and forced him out into the world. Here, through the voice, is the assurance of forgiveness. He feels lonely, and the voice says, *Behold, I am with you.* His future is full of uncertainty; and God says, *I . . . will keep you wherever you go, and will bring you back to this land* (v. 15). Can he endure the temptations that must lie ahead, and not repeat the abject failure of the past? God says, *I will not leave you until I have done that of which I have spoken to you* (v. 15).

The overwhelmed and awakening mind

Then Jacob awoke from his sleep and said, Surely the Lord is in this place; and I did not know it (v. 16).

We are meant, as we hear these awakening words of Jacob, to sense a thrill of unbelievable delight and surprise— that at such a low period in Jacob's life and fortunes God should have cared to break into his depression and scatter all the clouds; that so sinful a man as he should be spoken to and commissioned by God; that God so great and omnipresent should be able to draw so near to a person in one place; that such a dismal-looking locality should become itself for a moment so brilliantly transfigured into the gate of heaven!

There is also the beginning of a confession in these words, *I knew it not!* (v. 16 AV). He knows he should have known it could become so! He is confessing the prejudice of his previous mind-set. If he had had a fair and open mind to what he had been told about God even within the family circle in which he had felt so confined, then he could have known before it happened that it would be just like God to come in this way, with such grace, even to a place like this, to meet one like him.

Surely the Lord is in this place; and I knew it not (v. 16). We have them both here together—the thrill and excitement of an overwhelming new discovery, and the confession of the willful blindness that has kept us from discovering it till now. How often we are far too slow to believe that such a thing can happen, here and now, to such as us, in such a way! Which of us, before it really happened, would have been prepared to admit that through a visit to a local church, an approach to the Lord's Supper, the reading of the Bible, the hearing of a sermon—through all or any of these things, we could find ourselves indeed visited, spoken to, illuminated in mind, uplifted in heart and set on our way with new strength because we have met with God himself?

For a brief moment fear and awe seem to overwhelm all other feelings in Jacob—*And he was afraid, and said, 'How awesome is this place! This is none other than the house of God'* (v. 17). Such a sense of the nearness and presence of the Holy God often compelled others in the Bible to fall on their faces and worship.

The commitment

Then Jacob made a vow, saying, 'If God will be with me, and will keep me in this way that I go, and will give me bread to eat and clothing to wear, so that I come again to my father's house in peace, then the Lord shall be my God, and this stone, which I have set up for a pillow, shall be God's house; and of all that thou givest me I will give the tenth to thee' (vv. 20-2).

Jacob is not bargaining. Something quite transforming in character has begun to happen to him. Von Rad sums it up well: 'God's promise in verses 13-15 contained a great offer.

Jacob grasped the proffered hand and held drastically, i.e. he bound himself by a threefold vow to this saving act of God.'

Jacob has real difficulty in deciding exactly how best to express his gratitude. He is beginning to try to be a new person. He is trying genuinely to break with the defects that have marked his past life. Does he not in the presence of God remember with some shame the smooth, fulsome religious language which formerly too easily flowed from his tongue to deceive his father (cf. 27.20)? Therefore now he *must* mean business! He tries to save himself from any further hypocrisy by defining deeds rather than emotions. He says very simply: *The Lord shall be my God*. What more is needed? If we could all say this from the heart, our churches would be renewed. Then he adds that he will one day build a temple in this very place to God, and that he will pledge a tenth of his income for its upkeep. Surely this is a good, if awkward, effort! If we all gave this tenth, our churches would have all the resources they need for spectacular advance.

Though we must not underestimate what happened at Bethel, we must remember, however, that the degree of our human self-commitment to God at any one stage of our life is always imperfect. There are no degrees in the measure of God's self-commitment to us. He always gives himself totally and reveals himself without reserve. He never withholds what we can grasp and take. He is always ready to make the relationship between himself and us reflect the universal nature of his love in the cross. It is we, with our slowness to believe, who create the progressive stages that sometimes appear in our Christian lives. For Jacob, the experience at Bethel will prove to be only a first stage towards something much deeper that will take place when he is more ready to receive God's grace in a greater fullness.

To the Church at Laodicea, Jesus spoke: 'Behold, I stand at the door and knock; if anyone hears my voice and opens the door, I will come in to him and eat with him, and he with me' (Rev. 3.20). He, within, is always ready to eat with us. He is there, the guest now the host, ready to share everything with us as he eats with us: 'I will eat with him'. But what about 'he with me'? Here is where many of us, like Jacob, are so slow! We have heard his voice and opened the door, but sometimes we keep him waiting for a self-giving on our part to respond to his own.

14

The Sweet and the Bitter

GENESIS 29.1-30

Signs

When Jacob at last met *Rachel the daughter of Laban his mother's brother* (v. 10), he *wept aloud* (v. 11). It was not love at first sight which caused his expression of emotion (though this too was there). It was, rather, his exuberant joy after a series of remarkable happenings which to his mind had confirmed the vision he had been given at Bethel and the promises of the voice he had heard there.

During the long journey Jacob has had time to think coolly over the whole experience, and to ask how real it has been. One cannot build one's life only on what happens in a dream!—or was it more than a dream?

To prove to himself that the whole thing was more than a dream, no doubt Jacob craves to be given some concrete signs to help to assure him in the weariness and doubts that occasionally come to him—like Gideon (Judges 6.36 ff.) and others (Ps. 86.17) who will follow him later in the faith.

The signs that come to Jacob are as surprising as the vision. When he knows he is nearing Laban's neighbourhood he comes to a well. His mother has told him about the coincidences which happened when Abraham's servant Eleazar, praying for guidance, was led to the well near her old home (Gen. 24). There he met people who knew Laban. There at the same moment as they were speaking of him, she had come on the scene—the very woman the man had been seeking!

And now, for Jacob, as a sign from God confirming everything, the same sequence of guidance follows, exactly coinciding—except that Rachel is there now instead of Rebekah. No wonder Jacob weeps, and feels that God, having led him first to the gate of heaven, is now leading him to the gate of new life on earth too!

Joy!

And now he dares—and achieves—something quite out of the ordinary. He does it in the exuberance of his joy

He knows sheep. He has cared for them. He has learned much about their needs and ways in his father's homestead. These sheep round this well, he can see, are suffering greatly for lack of water. He challenges their shepherds about it. Why don't they care? They answer that their custom is to wait on, even in the heat, till everyone else has come, and then to roll the stone from the mouth of the well, together. Of course the sheep may be a little thirsty! 'Yes! Yes!' but— with a shrug of the shoulder—'We always do it this way!'

Wisely at first Jacob restrains himself from comment. But when Rachel arrives, he can no longer hold himself back. His desire to do something to register his joy over what God has done to him breaks through the bounds of normal wisdom for a moment and he attempts something quite rash and extravagant in its challenge to his strength. He goes down himself to the mouth of the well, and in front of the whole group he tackles the very stone which, they have affirmed, only a crowd of men can move. And there and then—we can call it a miracle either of sheer delight or of God!—an access of extraordinary strength is given to him. The stone is removed, and he waters the flock of his newly found cousin (v. 11). 'The joy of the Lord is your strength', said a later leader of Israel to his people (Neh. 8.10).

How changed is Jacob—a new man! What has happened to him has taken away all shyness and reserve, has enabled him to cut through the hampering customs and routine of the world around him. Can he not then, in everything that will face him, rise above what defeats other people and what would have defeated himself too, before? He will at least test the new power that has come, and will try surprising things! He must express the joy of his new liberty and hope in God! We shall never see Jacob so spontaneously happy, so liberated, as he is during the next few weeks; and indeed for the next few years.

How changed life always becomes for us when we are freshly sure that God has broken into our life and done wonderful things to make us glad! Of course, in the New Testament the same exuberant elation that Jacob felt was expressed in the presence of Jesus by those who came under his influence. We see it in the surprising and enthusiastic things that people like the woman with her precious box of ointment (Mark 14.3 ff.), or Zacchaeus with his cheque-book in his hand (Luke 19.1 ff.) did when they knew he had saved them from sin and from themselves. Our own Christian lives would be poor indeed if now and then we did not find ourselves attempting to surprise even ourselves and to cut through our own routine.

God is going to lead Jacob through a very long, dark and dangerous valley (Ps. 23.4).

None of the Patriarchs saw so evil days as he [remarked Bishop Hall]. His children (the staff of his old age) worried his soul to the death, Reuben proves incestuous, Judah adulterous, Dinah ravished, Simeon and Levi murderous, Er and Onan stricken dead, Joseph lost, Simeon imprisoned, Benjamin, the death of his mother, the father's right hand, endangered; himself driven by famine in his old age to die amongst the Egyptians, a people that held it abomination to eat with him.

But on the same way there are 'green pastures' and 'still waters' (Ps. 23.2), too, and undoubtedly the period which followed Jacob's arrival at the house of Laban, led there by Rachel, saw him through such a passage. He has fallen in with the right people to live with, and has met the right girl. He has made a deep impression on the man who holds the key to his domestic and financial future. The writer of the story deliberately dwells on the warmth of his welcome; the pleasant details of his first few years in which every hardship was lightened by his love for Rachel! All this—and the vision at Bethel too!

For God's people, the Sabbath was regarded as a period within ordinary time, given by God to be of quite special significance. It was the time of privileged rest amongst days of labour. It was a time for pausing in the midst of the hard battle of the other days. It contained within itself a foretaste of the joy and future destiny that would be at last fulfilled when the labour and the battle of the other days came to an end. In giving the Sabbath day to his people as part of the routine of this hard life on earth, God meant to ensure that the burden and heat and strife that took up the other days would be endurable till the glorious end foreshadowed in the Sabbath finally came.

When we review Jacob's life as a whole, we are justified in thinking of this particular period within it as a kind of distinct and prolonged 'Sabbath' period of joy and relaxation. This quiet pause in his life spent apart from the pressure of worldly conflict, of over-much business, allowed what was still echoing through his mind after Bethel to register more fully and deeply. The seed of the word of God was able to take root and establish itself and grow without being choked at its birth.

Laban

The sabbatical years ended when Jacob discovered Laban. Strangely, at first, he had trusted him and had felt especially favoured by him. After all, this was his mother's brother! He had met him just after his Bethel experience—when he was deeply impressionable and when God was opening him up to himself, to life with its opportunities, and to other people too.

Laban had certainly been attracted to Jacob at first. From the time he heard about the stone and the well, he had felt him to be his kind of man. He had proved far more capable in anything he had been asked to do than were the others around the place. But Laban saw people only as possible financial assets. Jacob was obviously a good one, and Laban could trade on his love for Rachel. His coming had enhanced her value enormously. Yet Leah, unwanted by anyone, was Laban's main problem. He thought out a plan to substitute one girl for the other on the wedding night and to trap Jacob into bed with her, so that he would have to take her too— with Rachel!

After the trap went off and Jacob had been irrevocably caught Laban put on an innocent air. Didn't Jacob know the law of the land he was living in? The elder daughter must always be taken before the younger. How could he really ever have imagined that he would get Rachel first! The idea had never entered Laban's mind: would a father do this?

The worst feature of the whole incident was that Laban

made it a huge and coarse public joke. He was himself obviously well respected and influential, and the wedding was a great local occasion. He loved to be at the centre of such entertainment. Others were privy to the joke as it was all being worked out. The laughs were enormous. Sadly, too, Leah must have at least assented, even if reluctantly. We have to remember this when we watch her more closely later.

Though today not many fathers are able, as crudely as he did, to conscript their children for their own selfish profit into the family business, we can nevertheless recognize Laban around us. We have the politician or businessman for whom everything must be subservient to economics. We have the entertainer who will make a spicy joke out of a human affair that can bring nothing but tragedy and bitterness to those most closely involved. We have the news-media man—no matter how cruelly it violates the intimacies of other people's lives, no matter whether it creates false impressions and divides families, no good story can be missed!

Yet, strangely, Laban can attract people. He is popular enough to be the centre of a large circle. He appears to be reliable and he can gain the confidence especially of the young and impressionable, who only find him out after his influence has damaged their trust in life and in people. He is all the more able to wield this measure of influence because he has been himself brought up in a tradition in which there is some true belief in God. Even though he himself has personally rejected the faith, he has retained a sufficient measure of the outward moral respectability required to be thought a 'good man' in his day.

If we shunned him more today, he might be less approved by others. Yet perhaps the reason why we do not do so is that there is so much of ourselves in him.

THE SWEET AND THE BITTER

The reckoning

The moment when Jacob wakes up to find that he has been deceived—that Leah is there instead of Rachel!—is almost as decisive as the moment when he awoke at Bethel. Then he had to reckon with God in the voice and the vision. Now he has to reckon with God in what Laban (and life itself) have done to him. For his uncle has done to him exactly what he himself did to his father and his brother: substituted one person for another by trickery and stealth. Here is one more in a series of coincidences in the way his life is being shaped—one set of circumstances corresponding exactly to another set.

He cannot fail to acknowledge the hand of the God of Bethel leading him on (see p. 89). He must acknowledge the accusing finger in the picture of himself written in the page of the book of life which is now opened before him by God. Under such an indictment he can find in himself no passion of righteous indignation with which to confront his human enemy.

Jacob does not try to think it out theologically—as we ourselves often try to do. Of course he blames Laban! Only in the evil mind of such a man could such an act of cynical human wickedness be hatched. God cannot have been the author of this cheap joke! But even though he knows himself to be in the hands of Laban; he knows that whatever evil God allows to touch his children is under his control, and that always, in whatever happens, they are subject to his fatherly care. He will live in future suspicious of the man who has cheated him so foully. But he will try to submit himself to the strange but trustworthy working of the hand of God. A psalmist later in Israel's history, no doubt under an experience similar to his, gave expression to his feelings: 'I am dumb, I do not open my mouth; for it is thou who hast done it' (Ps. 39.9).

He cannot break with Laban. He is too closely bound up

98

with the man, and Laban still has control of Rachel, whom Jacob will be allowed to marry when he has fully accepted Leah—though he will be bound down to serve for seven more years.

Now his chief task in life can begin: to build his home, to become the father of the people of God. It is not to be as he had hoped. But he still has in his mind the promise: 'By you and your descendants shall all the families of the earth bless themselves. Behold, I am with you and will keep you . . . for I will not leave you until I have done that of which I have spoken to you' (Gen. 28.14-15).

15

The Building of the House

GENESIS 29.31-30.24

Passion, strife, birth—and God!

The later historians of Israel looked on the birth of the twelve sons of Jacob as an important part of the plan which God was quite deliberately working out, even in its details, as he shaped the early life of their nation.

Even the number, it was believed, had some significance. For twelve tribes, one from each of Jacob's sons, were to be brought by Moses out of Egypt. They were to be organized by him into a political and cultural unity, as a nation. They were to be led into the promised land and settled there under Joshua. They were to be protected and kept together as one nation during the period of the Judges. When the kingdom set up by David later split, and the northern tribes disap-

99

peared into captivity, always the hope remained that some-how their number, twelve, would be restored when the destiny of the nation was finally realized. And Jesus, claiming himself to fulfil the promises and to be the founder of the New Israel, chose twelve that they might become his witnesses and found his Church. Therefore, in and through all that happens in this story before us now, God is regarded as engaged on one of his most special of all works—the birth and early nurture of these twelve!

Yet it is a dreadfully complicated and sad story of human weakness and superstition. When we read it, as von Rad remarks, we feel we are taking a journey through a 'truly unedifying thicket of passions and naked human character-istics'.

The marriage begins, of course, with a rivalry between the two wives which may have had a long previous history. But the intensity of the envy grows when the babies come, one after the other for Leah—four of them (29.31-5)! Poor Rachel! *Give me children, or I shall die* (30.1)! she cries to Jacob. She becomes so jealous that her maid is brought in to help her in the situation.

It was an accepted custom for a servant to bear a child by the husband, in place of the wife. The child was described as being born 'on the knees' of the wife (30.4; of *Abraham*, p. 53). The intensity of Rachel's feeling against her sister is revealed in the names she gives to the two children born in this way. She feels vindicated by God when the first arrives. To celebrate the second birth she says, *I have wrestled with my sister, and have prevailed*, and put the phrase into the baby's name (30.8). Yet Leah forges ahead, bringing in Zilpah, her maid, who bears two more on her side (30.9-13). Then the child-bearing race stops for a while.

One day Leah's Reuben finds mandrakes in a field. These were strong-smelling roots that were regarded as having aphrodisiac qualities. The fact that a mere child brought such a thing to his mother makes us realize that even he at this age had been led to understand that it was only by having babies that his mother felt she had any status and use, for she feared that her husband had no longer any desire for her.

But Rachel hears of the find, pleads and bargains with Leah. She will even relax her firm hold of Jacob for a night or two to have these mandrakes (30.14-16). It starts off a new series of pregnancies—two more boys for Leah, and then a daughter Dinah (30.17-21). Then *God remembered Rachel* (30.22), and Joseph is born—the eleventh boy. One more is yet to come to reach the completed twelve. Rachel seems to sense that one is missing and prays that it may be her joy to bear him: *May the Lord add to me another son!* (30.24). Her prayer is heard and answered later with Benjamin.

The sisters are moved by jealousy and anger. In their scheming they resort to strange current medical superstitions, sordid bargaining, and legalized pretence with servants as concubines. Yet in the midst of it all, God is at work—building the house of Jacob!

The shadow of impoverishment?

It is clearly brought out later in the story that Jacob in a few years' time is to find that he has on his hands a deeply divided family of boys—who seem to have failed to grasp with any fullness what it means to serve the God of their fathers. Most of them are untamed and untameable—always naturally inclining to disloyalty, brutality, adultery and murder. They soon begin to take control even of the home situation in ways that gradually break Jacob's heart.

Finally it is God who has to tame them. The whole story of Joseph is indeed the story of how God, later on, through the bitter discipline of years of suffering under harsh circumstances, brings them finally to true repentance and a right mind.

101

THE BUILDING OF THE HOUSE

We are justified in finding that many of the seeds of these later tragedies in Jacob's life were sown at this period when the children were young, some of them in their cradles and some in their infancy. It is hard to assess the blame for this. The circumstances were overwhelmingly difficult.

Yet this period is Jacob's time of opportunity. God is at work; Jacob too must be at work. God has created for him a family situation full of entirely new and great possibilities—open and waiting for him to take new leadership. Since God had 'opened the womb' for each birth to take place he will no less surely open the mind of each growing child to receive another kind of seed. Jacob must sow truth so that God can bring about healthy mental and spiritual growth. Jacob's self-giving to each child around him, as an earthly father, must reflect something of God's own care for each, so that each individual can begin to glimpse what it means to have a heavenly father as well as an earthly one.

There are hints in the story that Jacob is more responsible than his wives for falling short. He compares badly even with his own father. Isaac at least prayed with his wife in her distress at her barrenness, but Jacob became angry when Rachel turned to him for support (30.2). Each of his wives appears to be alone before God in her prayers and praises. Did he give them no leadership—and was family religion at this stage simply left to become a personal and private matter for each? It may be significant that whereas Abraham gave names to both Ishmael and Isaac, Jacob takes no part in naming any of these eleven boys. The only point at which he seems to exert his influence is to make clear his love for Rachel and his distaste for Leah, and his preference soon registers in the minds of his growing family. Otherwise he does not seem to want responsibility. The women, unable to agree, pull him now one way and now another way. He does not seem to be 'at home' when he is at home.

Those of us who have our families beginning to grow around us are meant to notice these things. A noted Scots preacher took a text from the book of Job: 'when my children were about me' (Job 29.5). His first heading was: 'When our children are about us, they should be about us.'

Leah

We have to try to understand Leah if we are going to understand Jacob. Yet we find that she becomes enigmatic and haunting as we look at the faint lines of the portrait drawn of her in this story. She reminds us of the Mona Lisa!

The more we study her, the more we come to like her—and to pity Jacob for his own 'weak eyes'. Of course, externally she is nothing in comparison with Rachel. Something about her eyes seems to spoil her appearance (cf. 29.17). They are 'dull' (NEB) with 'no sparkle' (JB) about them.

Indeed, she must be held to blame to some extent for permitting herself to be substituted for Rachel in the first place. But the account in the Bible deliberately covers this over by giving us no evidence of how much she was *willingly* involved. If Laban tricked Jacob, he could have tricked Leah, too, even more easily, for undoubtedly in contrast to her future husband she was basically naive. We can only judge her character by the attitude she took in her sufferings and by the prayers she offered to God in her great affliction:

and Leah conceived and bore a son, and she called his name Reuben; for she said, 'Because the Lord has looked upon my affliction; surely now my husband will love me.' She conceived again and bore a son, and said, 'Because the Lord has heard that I am hated, he has given me this son also'; and she called his name Simeon. Again she conceived and bore a son, and said, 'Now this time my husband will be joined to me because I have borne him three sons'; therefore his name was called Levi. And she conceived again and bore a son, and said,

'This time I will praise the Lord', therefore she called his name *Judah; then she ceased bearing* (29.32-5).

Luther is one of Leah's champions, and he underlines the contrast we find at this stage in their marriage, between her and the envious and much less prayerful Rachel (cf. 30.1-3). He is all sympathy for the elder girl:

> She is not beautiful, not pleasing. No, she is odious and hated. There the poor girl sits . . . Rachel gives herself airs before her . . . 'I am the lady of the house,' she thought. Moreover if she (Leah) gave any orders to the household they said, 'Why do you give me orders? Rachel and Jacob do not care for you'.

Luther also points out that this incident shows us how God loves to lavish his gifts and blessings especially on what is despised. 'For what the world, and even saintly people like Jacob and Rachel, throw away, this he gathers up, and it is altogether sacred to him,' for 'God . . . has regard solely and in a special manner for what is despised and cast off, just as Christ himself was on the Cross.'

Therefore because he saw that Leah was despised, God determined to make her the centre of the life of the home and the source of the blessing that the others must seek and find. It was when God *saw* that she was despised that *therefore* he blessed her (29.31-2)! 'Poor Leah', writes Luther, 'was sad and pained that she was despised by her lord. But listen to Moses who says, THE LORD SAW etc. No one else sees it. God has regard for and blesses the downcast, weeping, odious, and saddened woman, but he humbles the one who is proud.'

Jacob has to become humble enough to see that not only has God concealed his blessing in Leah but that he, Jacob, has also to find his future hidden in his relationship with her. No matter in what direction he is inclined by his personal disposition and taste, he is meant to see that God has made Leah rather than Rachel the kingpin of the home.

From Leah, Sarna points out, 'issued the tribes of Levi and Judah, which shared between them the spiritual and temporal hegemony of Israel, providing the two great dominating institutions of the biblical period, the priesthood and the Davidic monarchy.' As we look further to the beginning of the New Testament we find that it is Judah, Leah's son, who is given a place in the genealogy of Jesus Christ.

Jacob is therefore meant not only to accept her but also to serve, honour and protect her. There is no way in which he can find peace or a future in bypassing her. She is the stone set there in front of him for him to make both the foundation-stone at the start of his home-building and the headstone of the corner at the end, or his life-work will be in vain.

Leah, Rachel and ourselves

Jacob's attitude to Leah in the home is defined for us in verses 30 and 31. The first observes that he loved Rachel more than Leah; the second says that *Leah was hated*. Other modern translations tone down the word 'hated', and we accept that of the Jerusalem Bible which says that she *'was neglected'*.

When we ask why, we accept Luther's suggestion that Jacob was too proud.

Can we not understand him? Rachel, he felt, offered him self-fulfilment. She nearly always gave him pleasure. Leah demanded self-sacrifice. She stood for the way that none of us naturally takes to, for the kind of self-denial Christ calls for from those who would follow him. Though Jacob's future lay in this way of self-denial, he sought it where he believed he would find only self-fulfilment.

If we try to analyse the situation more psychologically we may dwell on the fact that Leah also humbled him because she reminded him acutely of the guilt of his past life, for God had made her, on their encounter at the wedding, a symbol of his guilt in the affair of Esau. If we wish to probe the situation more theologically we can dwell on the comment of a modern writer that in his neglect of Leah, it is ultimately against God's decree that 'Jacob's pent-up passion bounds'. There is something in us all that leads us in such a way and Jacob was no stranger to it.

For most of us, however, Leah is a reminder that God often places for us, at the centre of things, some fact of life like this, something it is hard for us to accommodate to and to deal with adequately. We are tempted to reject or neglect it rather than to face and accept it, because such acceptance would involve us in too big a measure of self-sacrifice and humiliation. Yet as with Jacob, our ability to fulfill the will of God, and our hope of being blessed by God, are closely bound up with whether or not we can honestly face up to the challenge he gives to our self-centredness and pride.

Paul had his thorn in the flesh. It was there, always haunting and, he felt, hindering him. Three times he prayed to God to take it away. He called it 'a messenger of Satan, to harass me' (2 Cor. 12.7). But he did not find peace till he heard God tell him to cease resisting, to obey, to find strength in his weakness and glorify God through submission to his infirmity.

Lazarus at the gate of the rich man, in the story Jesus told, was rather like Leah in Jacob's house. He was neighbour to Dives the rich man, though he was placed at his gate rather than in his bed. Dives, however, despised Lazarus and passed him by daily. It was only when it was too late that he woke up in hell to see Lazarus there in heaven, and to realize how much he needed him (Luke 16.20ff.)! Even if Jacob could not take Leah as a beloved wife, she was his neighbour. It was God who had placed her in the house and who intended that Jacob's future should depend on his finding this out.

Does accepting Leah necessarily mean that we exclude Rachel? The story says No! It does not condemn Jacob for his first choice. What can possibly be wrong in a love that can make a man serve fourteen years for a woman? Let us by all means seek the desires of our heart before God. Let us beseech him even more than Paul did to take away the thorn in the flesh! Let us rejoice in our youth and in all that it can bring.

But if Leah, in spite of all our prayers and hopes, is there—to be concerned about and cared for—presenting us with issues in life that cannot be neglected if we are to have any future before God, then woe to us if we try to solve our problems the easy way! Only by caring for Leah can Rachel ever become truly ours too. It was Leah who lived on with Jacob to become his stay and support in the harder days to come.

16

The Six Years and the Seven Days

GENESIS 30.25-31.55

Towards disentanglement

In our theological seminary in the United States we sometimes found that post-graduate students from the Far East who brought their wives and young families with them found themselves in acute difficulty when it came to leaving for home. It happened especially if their stay had been lengthened by a period of post-graduate work. They found that their children had settled down very quickly—adopting

firm attitudes and putting down strong roots. Then sometimes the parents *had* to stay!

It began to happen this way with Jacob. He realized one
day that he was in danger of becoming too much entangled
there in Paddan-aram, amongst the sheep and the goats, the
kindred and the ways of life. The sense of this danger, and
the longing to be free, came with especial force when Joseph
was born—his own special child—of Rachel! What kind of
future did he really want to offer this one? The question
gradually applied itself to the others also.

Other considerations, too, were there in his mind. Surely
enough was enough! Had he not served Laban long, fulfilled
his contracts more faithfully than such a man deserved? Had
not God so blessed his work that the man had become rich?
He made his desires and his mind known:

> *Send me away that I may go to my own home and country.*
> *Give me my wives and children for whom I have served*
> *you . . . you yourself know . . . for you had little before I*
> *came, and it was increased abundantly; and the Lord has*
> *blessed you wherever I turned. But now when shall I provide*
> *for my own household also* (30.25–30)?

Significantly, it was only when he began to want to go that
he began to realize how far he had become subject to the
family environment and to the will of Laban. His uncle's
answer sounded pleasant, but behind all the outward affa-
bility of the moment there was a firm determination either
to keep him where he was or to let him go only at the cost of
everything he wanted to take with him. He himself could go
when he wanted, but his wives and children belonged to the
family group and were actually unalienable local property.

At first Laban avoided saying such a thing bluntly. He
admitted his debt to Jacob and diverted the discussion by
suggesting a new wage agreement. It was to take a full six
years before the situation developed sufficiently for Jacob to
make a move towards the settlement of the basic problem.

The passage under present discussion gives the story of these six years. At the end of them a crisis occurred in which Jacob nearly lost everything. There was a desperate flight and pursuit lasting seven days, then a final round-up of Jacob and his helpless family by Laban, and a miraculous deliverance by God.

When we read through the whole story we are meant to see that God was as much there at the start of this final phase of Jacob's life as he was in the crisis at the end. The six years are the story of a miracle of disentanglement no less extraordinary than the final miracle of deliverance. The whole account of the six years and seven days is meant indeed to be read as a catalogue of miracle.

A catalogue of miracle

The miracle of disentanglement begins in the field. Jacob refuses to make a fresh wage settlement with Laban and insists on a productivity deal. He offers terms which seem to be wholly in Laban's favour.

Most of Laban's flocks, whether of sheep or goats, are as we would expect normally to see them, white sheep and unicoloured goats, brown or black. Only occasionally does there appear the blackish lamb or the striped or speckled spotted goat—and when such animals give birth, their offspring usually revert to normal colours. Jacob suggests that as his wages he should simply take whatever among the flocks are born with these abnormalities in colour (30.31-4).

Laban agrees, but before the bargain period begins he proves his meanness by removing from the flocks every sheep and goat that is of the type Jacob wants, leaving him only with the breeding animals that seem most likely to give normally-coloured kids and lambs (30.35).

But Jacob has in mind an ingenious plan. He has learned to believe that in the animal world the offspring of a mother will acquire certain characteristics through what happens at the time of copulation. If at the time of breeding a certain shock can be given, or certain visual impressions are received by the mother-to-be, then when the birth occurs these will be registered in the colour of the coats of the young. Jacob, therefore, devises a scheme to produce such an effect on a large scale amongst his sheep and goats. This gives us the key to the account we have of his peeling rods, putting them in the watering troughs so that the effect would register at the moment of breeding when the flocks came to drink. But Jacob makes sure that he does this only in the case of the strong and best animals. He avoids giving the treatment to the weaker animals, which he allows to breed for Laban (30.37–42)! Thus Jacob becomes wealthy—an important step towards his independence (30.43).

Of course the whole scheme required skill and took infinite care and hard work. But we are told by Jacob himself that the inspiration to do it came from God (31.12), that it worked only because God himself made it work (31.8–9). Moreover, in whatever happened in the field God was at work not only enriching Jacob but separating his wealth from that of Laban; and giving it a distinctive mark so that when the time came for parting there could be no recrimination or suspicion. We are meant to notice the irony of the fact that Laban himself was inspired by God to inaugurate the disentanglement when he separated any animal over which there might be future dispute or controversy and put such under his sons' care, at a great distance from Jacob himself (30.36).

While all this was taking place during these six years in the field a miracle no less remarkable was taking place in Jacob's home. We suddenly discover at the end of this period that, after thirteen years of life with his wives, in spite of his work and toil for them, his marriage to them, his sharing with them in rearing and bringing up his family, Jacob is not in the end certain that he has enough personal hold on both to persuade them to go with him. This need not surprise us when we see often today how little can be left, after thirteen years, of the ideal marriage—even with a Rachel involved!—and even with a large and dependent growing family. We have to remember, too, that the grip of 'the father's house' on a married woman in those days was more powerful than we experience today, and that the strength of the ties that bound his wives to Jacob was weakened by their being two rather than one.

Therefore we see Jacob, not fully aware of what has been taking place in the mind of his wives and children, suddenly growing anxious, and overcome by a feeling of utter loneliness at the very moment when the call comes for him to go (cf. 31.3-4).

Will his wives really go with him? Or is it to be God's will that he should sacrifice everything and go—alone? The call comes at a time when everything else is threatening too. Stories are being circulated by the *sons of Laban*, a powerful group, no doubt jealous of Jacob's too-close relationship with their father, that Jacob has stolen his wealth and theirs, that he deceived Laban when they entered their agreement over the flocks (31.1). Moreover Laban himself is being affected by such talk, and he is the man who matters. Jacob begins to wonder how deeply such stories and such a developing situation have affected his influence on his own home.

We have the picture of a depressed and very lonely Jacob calling Leah and Rachel to a meeting in the fields. We sense his nervousness in the apologetic way in which he begins to address them, explaining his innocence over against all the rumours they have been hearing, claiming that all along he has been trying to obey God and do what is right in an atmosphere in which trust has become impossible through their father's unreliability. His arguments are not too clear, but the main drift of his appeal is obvious: the God of Bethel has helped him and has now told him that it is time to go. Do they believe enough in him and in God to come?

111

THE SIX YEARS AND THE SEVEN DAYS

Jacob finds that God has already been speaking to his wives about the whole matter, even before he has made his speech. They have already grasped the situation, understood the issues and made the choice between him and Laban—*whatever God has said to you do* (31.16)!

His new discovery of what God has done put so much heart into him that without a moment's delay things are hurriedly gathered, the camels are mounted and the flight is started. His haste, however, and his foolish attempt to *outwit Laban* (31.20) lead him into disaster. Laban and his kinsmen, spurred on by anger at being slighted, overtake him, and Laban is determined on revenge. *But God came to Laban the Aramean in a dream by night, and said to him, 'Take heed that you say not a word to Jacob, either good or bad'* (31.24). This is the third miracle in our catalogue—a miracle in the camp of the enemy!

The fourth miracle meets the most dangerous situation of all. It takes place under Jacob's eyes, but he does not know at the time either the danger he is in, or how God is helping him out of it! Rachel proves herself incredibly foolish. Why does she do it? Perhaps, sharing Jacob's elation at the moment of their pledge to defy Laban and go with him, she can not resist having a last jab at her father where she knows it will hurt. At any rate she consults nobody and steals his *teraphim*—private household gods, revered at home and consulted when oracles were needed. They were of great religious significance and precious as heirlooms from the past. Jacob is shocked that Laban should think any of his household could stoop to such a theft: *If found, let the culprit die, he swears* (31.32).

God alone can save in a juncture such as this—and he does so again! The writer expects us to see the twinkle in God's eye and understand that the Almighty has a glorious sense of humour when he saves his holy family. Rachel is in a state of menstrual 'uncleanness'. She sits down on the package they are all looking for. No one will dare to disturb

112

her. Her action enables her to express her total contempt for the superstition she is forsaking, and it provides a story that will last as long as Israel's history lasts, to show that false 'gods' are always forced to hide and to humiliate themselves and to remain dumb when God is busy in the field of life!

'The Mighty One of Jacob!'

Time and again in the Psalms and elsewhere God is called the 'God of Jacob', and one of the psalmists twice in a Psalm calls him 'the Mighty One of Jacob' (Ps. 132. 2, 5). Even in reviewing the short passage before us now in this chapter, we can begin to understand what led him to such a title.

This is indeed the God under whose providence and control we, who follow Jacob, continually live our lives and experience our own contemporary miracles! He is the God whose powerful help in seeing us through our earthly problems is often gradual, often hidden but no less sure and wonderful for that. He is the God who knows our financial needs, understands farmers' markets, cattle-breeding and stock exchange, and can work such things for our help when and how he wills. He is the God who not only brings people together in marriage but can bind them closer together in loyal and lasting love of one for another so that death alone can part them. He is the God who within a home can 'turn the hearts of the fathers to their children, and children to their fathers' (Mal. 4.6; Luke 1.17), so that they too begin to share in the same loyal love. He is the God who, even when we have justly deserved the anger of others, can calm the desire for revenge and restrain the evil that could have been launched against us. He is the God who can take control of the dreadful consequences that the crazy impulses of one member of a family can bring upon the whole group, and who can suddenly flash into a mind an idea that can save in threatened disaster. And he does it all in such a quiet and steady way that we hardly know he is doing it. Sometimes

113

the miracle takes place before our eyes, and we do not notice it (cf. 31.32 ff.). Our times are in his mighty hands!

We sometimes have to admit that what we prefer to call our 'involvement' in the world around us can become too often a bondage to it. Many of us, and our families too, become hindered from being as faithful in our service and witness to God as we once hoped to be. We are held back, not because we suddenly lapse into the kind of sin that took David or Peter by surprise (2 Sam. 11.1ff.; Luke 22.55ff.) but by a much more gradual process. We simply become caught up into new attitudes and new developing ways of life, ourselves growing into them as the family grows. Such things as money, status, popularity and 'push' begin to matter more than they used to matter, for others are involved besides ourselves. We no less than Jacob come to need the same work of disentanglement—in the hands of his mighty God!

The common sense of Laban

In the Bible God sometimes uses strange teachers in the education of his favoured children. Abraham had to sit at the feet first of the King of Egypt, and then of the King of Gerar, in order to be taught lessons in common sense and ethics (12.18ff.; 20.8ff.). Now Jacob has to learn the same kind of lessons from his uncle Laban. Rogue though he was, and insincere though much of his language was, Laban, indeed, we have to remember, also professed to follow the God of Abraham (31.53) and was in touch with good moral tradition.

Jacob needed Laban's reproach: *What have you done, that you have cheated me, and carried away my daughters like captives of the sword? Why did you flee secretly, and cheat me, and did not tell me, so that I might have sent you away with mirth and songs, with tambourine and lyre (31.26-7)?*

Laban is laying his finger on what has always been a bad

114

GENESIS 30.25–31.55

fault in Jacob: his inability to deal fairly and openly with
what is past, to face frankly and to settle the accounts it
renders. His nephew has to be made aware that the problems
of life are never to be solved by flight, evasion of issues and
stealth. He has to learn that, whatever our circumstances,
the power of God can enable us to adopt policies in dealing
with people that are open and frank, that enable us to part
company with them, when the time comes, with decency
and honour.

The God of the Bible is the 'God of peace' (1 Cor. 14.33;
Heb. 13.20). The greatest of all the miracles he wants to do
for all of us is to clear up the past, whatever the cost, to pay
debts, to make possible forgiveness and new life. Therefore
he wants us, as much as we are able, to clean up things
behind us, to settle our outstanding accounts with others,
both mentally and in other ways. 'Make friends quickly with
your accuser, while you are going with him to court', said
Jesus (Matt. 5.25). There will, of course, be a last, inevitable
reckoning, but it is much better to settle the debt now! 'Owe
no one anything, except to love one another', says Paul
(Rom. 13.8). God cares that we leave behind us, where we
have been about on earth, the good will that accompanies
those who belong to the God of peace.

We note the frank interchange of feeling into which
Laban's blustering example leads Jacob (31.26ff., 36ff.). It
is a step towards ultimate reconciliation, that offences,
imaginary or otherwise, should be brought into the open;
and even if amity is not finally reached it helps even a little
at times, to 'have it out'. Jacob finds that Laban is far more
ready to listen than he had ever imagined.

We note the covenant which is initiated by Laban. It
sounds like a non-aggression and boundary agreement
between future nations. There is something shrewd about
this old man. Even friends need to have the limits of their
liberty with each other well defined.

The ancient proverb is known: we should deal lawfully with our friends, that we may not afterwards be obliged to go to law with them [writes Calvin]. From whence arise so many legal broils, except that everyone is more liberal towards himself, and more niggardly towards others than he ought to be? Therefore, for the purpose of achieving concord, firm compacts are necessary, which may prevent injustice on one side or the other.

Laban's rather beautiful parting prayer, *The Lord watch between you and me, while we are absent one from the other* (31.49), is a prayer not for protection when aggression has started, but a prayer to be kept from devising any harm, thoughtlessly or deliberately. In the end his affection is stirred as he sees them all depart, and he expresses genuine concern for the future of his daughters (31.50). Let us give honour where honour is due.

17

Peniel

GENESIS 32.1-29

Mahanaim

Jacob went on his way and the angels of God met him (v. 1), *and when Jacob saw them he said, 'This is God's army!'*. We are told that he called the place of this new vision *Mahanaim*, which means 'two camps' (v. 2).

Obviously, at the moment it happened, Jacob took it that this vision was meant to bring assurance that he would be protected from the new danger which lay immediately ahead of him. These angels looked like an army of God, gathered in the field of heaven to be on his side. 'God is placing his visible protection before the eyes of Jacob', says Calvin. Up till now he had been able to think of only one camp—that of Esau. He had believed his brother was there blocking his way ahead, armed, waiting possibly to destroy him. He was soon to send messengers to see whether some kind of truce was possible, and they would return to confirm his worst fears (vv. 3-6). But now he knows that there are at least two camps (v. 2)! For God, too, in the midst of war preparations around his people has set up his own field headquarters (Zech. 9.8).

Some commentators think that Jacob saw in his mind's eye two heavenly camps, one behind and one before him. He had good cause to attribute his deliverance from Laban to an army of God. Now he knows there is another army prepared to clear the way before him. The angels round about us (Ps. 34.7)! It was an inspiring thought in the mind of a later prophet, that the people of God on their return journey out of exile into the promised land would have such an experience: 'For you shall not go out in haste, and you shall not go in flight, for the Lord will go before you, and the God of Israel will be your rear guard' (Isa. 52.12).

Is Jacob, in this vision, being encouraged to think back on the vision he had at Bethel before he left the land? That was full of angels. Now, as he enters the land again, there is a second vision—also full of angels! Is he meant now to think of himself as especially back amongst angels when he returns to the promised land? God has certainly been with him during his twenty years of exile. But now he is returning to a place unique in the mind of God and uniquely under the care of God—the place, indeed, in which heaven is to be nearer earth than in any other land, in which dreams and visions, such as he himself has experienced, will never fail to be given to the human mind. He is returning to the land

117

in which even the angels who are conscripted by God to protect his people within it will finally be filled with wonder at the work that is being done there (1 Pet. 1.12) and will fill heaven and even earth with joy as they see it happening (Luke 2.13f.).

Planning and prayer

Our next glimpse of Jacob comes when he hears that Esau has rejected his offer of a truce and is advancing with four hundred men. He is *greatly afraid and distressed* (v. 7). 'Jacob's reaction is characteristically energetic,' writes Kidner. 'He plans, 7, 8—prays, 9-12—plans, 13-21—prays 22-32—plans, 33.1-3.'

His first plan is to divide his company into two, so that they cannot all be destroyed at once. The recorded prayer which follows is worthy to be a model for all our praying. Thankfully he reminds God of his covenant with Abraham (v. 9), of his personal promise to Jacob himself in which it is implied that he will be seen through this particular crisis (v. 9). He sincerely confesses his unworthiness (v. 10), makes a clear and detailed description of his position (v. 10), tells God exactly the danger he wishes to avert (v. 11), asks for help, and ends up again reminding God of the salvation he has promised for all mankind (v. 12).

He then elaborates on the plans he has already made. He selects from his cattle and sheep a large present for Esau. This has to be sent on ahead in an attempt to mollify his brother's anger. He divides it into droves. Each drove has to follow the other at a distance. The leader of each drove, when he is accosted, has humbly to tell Esau that these are for him, to assure him of his brother's love and tell him that there are more to come. Surely Esau's anger will gradually abate when he sees such a token of sorrow and esteem!

No more . . . 'Jacob'!

Undoubtedly Jacob, left alone, prays again. But his planning and praying are suddenly interrupted by an experience which takes up most of the hours of waiting. What God accomplished with Jacob during that short space of time was decisive for his own future, and the account of it has been preserved in detail because those who followed him found it of great importance. Certainly it does not eclipse what happened to him at Bethel. Yet through it God finished his work begun there. During the experience God makes his intention with Jacob clear: *Your name shall no more be called Jacob, but Israel* (v. 28). Jacob is to be given a new name, and is thus to become in heart and attitude a new man.

His progress has so far fallen short. He is not yet the man God wants him to be. The last great step has not been taken. He has not yet become a man like Abraham with whom God, in the end, was well pleased because he would withhold nothing from his maker (cf. Ch. 22). Jacob has to be made such a man before he is allowed to enter the promised land to follow again in Abraham's steps. What has been wrong with Jacob that such a change is needed? We have had cause to admire him for the burning desire he has always felt in his heart and mind for God, his kingdom and his promises. But he has always tended to take the wrong way as he has sought to secure all these things. Instead of being a man of simple faith in God's word, he has always tended to be 'Jacob' in this battle—too clever in his striving and scheming, too basically self-reliant, too prone to substitute works for faith, cleverness for insight! What he specially needs at this moment, therefore, is to be taught how to *strive with God and with men* (v. 28) so as to prevail and to have what he is seeking so ardently. He needs to be taught to be *no longer . . . Jacob* (v. 28).

119

The divine assailant

The first thing God has to do is to teach him in no uncertain way *where* his main problem in life now lies. Here he is, facing a great crisis in his life. He is acting as if the chief problem before him is simply his quarrel with Esau. It has not entered his mind that there may be an even more serious and urgent quarrel between himself and God that has to be given priority in the settlement of his affairs. For here has been another great fault that has marred his life: he has always tended, in the midst of life's problems, to put off dealing straightforwardly with God about them, as long as he can deal cleverly and efficiently with men. He must learn that he has to deal with God about life first.

Therefore God himself has to break into his affairs and take him to task, before he can even reach Esau for the next battle. This is our most important clue to the story before us. Jacob finds himself encountered by one who seems to be an assailant:

> *And Jacob was left alone; and a man wrestled with him until the breaking of the day. When the man saw that he did not prevail against Jacob, he touched the hollow of his thigh; and Jacob's thigh was put out of joint as he wrestled with him. Then he said, 'Let me go, for the day is breaking.' But Jacob said, 'I will not let you go, unless you bless me.' And he said to him, 'What is your name?' And he said, 'Jacob'. Then he said, 'Your name shall no more be called Jacob, but Israel, for you have striven with God and with men, and have prevailed.' Then Jacob asked him, 'Tell me, I pray, your name.' But he said, 'Why is it that you ask my name?' And there he blessed him (vv. 24-29).*

We shall not be able to interpret this incident adequately if we think of it as describing a struggle carried on by Jacob, at a time of deep introspection, with his own inner nature. Nor will it yield anything if we imagine the 'man' to be the

120

'creation of his fevered brain', or a demon, or a 'river god'. The story yields its only intelligible message within the whole context in which it is told if we regard the incident as an intense struggle between Jacob and God himself. The antagonist is certainly referred to as a *man* and is later (by Jacob) spoken of as an angel (Gen. 48.16). But as 'man' or 'angel', he acts as God and represents God. Jacob says at the end of the incident: 'I have seen God face to face' (v. 30).

The experience somehow involved his physical being, and it marked him physically for life (v. 32). The divine assailant found him hard to overcome, and the struggle was prolonged. Even God's angelic power is baffled for a time by human stubbornness! Is this a foreshadowing of the ultimate truth that God has to involve himself in agony in order to overcome human resistance? Yet we have to say also that what prolonged the struggle was the concern to be gentle— not to hurt more than faithful friendship required.

Jacob had to be broken. As David discovered, centuries later, it is the broken and contrite heart that God loves (Ps. 51.17). Therefore, before he fills Jacob with new life, he has to be made empty. Before he is made rich he has to be made poor. We have to note, however, that the humiliation is finally brought about by a mere *touch* in the right place at the right time, for God understands even the human game of wrestling better than his opponent—and Jacob is soon helpless (v. 25).

Finally there has to be one more touch from God, one more test. 'What is your name?' (v. 27) asks the stranger. Of course, God already knows! But Jacob has to be compelled to speak it with shame. He realizes now that the name 'Jacob' sums up all the features of his past life, of the futility of which he is now becoming most conscious, the shame of which is now causing him grief. He has now to make his confession by admitting before God that this has indeed been his true nature—*Jacob*!

'Strong against God'

Jacob begins to change his mind about his 'adversary' before he reaches the stage of having to confess his own 'name'. When the touch dislocates his thigh he begins to realize that his situation is desperate. His pain is such that he can not even stand unless his assailant holds him up. Then he begins to discover that the one who is holding him so firmly is not an assailant at all but the divine friend who can give him everything he needs.

And now he is in a position to discover a new way to pray—a new way to seek divine grace and divine response. It is a way he has never really tried before, but God is teaching it to him now! For there is only one attitude he can take as he hangs there, broken, in the arms of God. He discovers that he can hold on to God, driven by the desperation of his weakness, and that this is a better way of prevailing than if he tries to fight God with his strength. Instead of resisting God any more he now begins to cling.

It is when he begins to cling to God with his weakness, in this completely new and determined way, that he discovers himself to be 'strong against God'. God is now responding to him. Indeed, he knows now that this is the kind of prayer God cannot refrain from answering—the kind of prayer to hear which God has actually brought such weakness upon him. Now he has learned the way to *ask*, out of his desperate need, what he used to *strive* to attain because he thought he had some strength.

Because he has made this discovery, he is given, on the spot, a new name. The Jerusalem Bible helps us better than other translations to understand the important 28th verse: *Your name shall no longer be Jacob, but Israel*, God says to him, *because you have been strong against God, you shall prevail against men*. The characteristic of the man who has this new name *Israel* is to be always, from now on, one who clings to God, trusting only in what God has promised and seeking only what God has promised, but strong in the certainty that he will have it, for himself and all others, because God has promised and because he makes human strength perfect in weakness.

Because his naturally divided make-up (cf. p. 60f.) has been so broken up in the hands of God, his heart can now at last become united (cf. Ps. 86.11) in the expression of one intense and desperate desire. He spells it out in quite definite and concrete terms. He asks for God's blessing, whatever it involves, whatever it will cost: *I will not let you go unless you bless me* (v. 26). It is a request to be enabled to have life from now on always in God's companionship, always under God's direction—a life at last like that of the blessed Abraham!

He also wants to know more about the source of such a gift, and about how it is to come to him. After God has asked him for his own name, he dares to ask God, in all humility: *Tell me, I pray, your name* (v. 29). He is trembling to *know* more, and he believes it cannot be sinful to want such knowledge.

Jacob receives the blessing: *And he blessed him* (v. 29)—but with the name it is different. The one who has already said, *Let me go, for the day is breaking* (v. 26), now says '*Why is it that you ask my name?*' (v. 29). It is his last word. The day begins to break and Jacob is left by himself. This prayer for the 'name' is not answered. But it is not denied. It will begin to be answered in God's good time. Later, Moses and other prophets will begin to hear preliminary hints of the answer which Jacob so fervently sought. But it will not be truly known till it is fully known in Jesus. How else could God speak it?

123

When God closes in

Of course, this story of Peniel is much more than a story from the history of Jacob.

> It contains experiences of faith [comments von Rad] that extend from the most ancient period down to the time of the narrator; there is charged to it something of the result of the entire divine history into which Israel was drawn . . . as it is now related it is clearly transparent as a type of that which Israel experienced from time to time with God. Israel has here presented its entire history with God almost prophetically as such a struggle until the breaking of the day!

The prophet Hosea, centuries later than Jacob, interpreted the story to his own contemporaries in this light. He said that Jacob's way of sinning had always been a characteristic of their nation's way of sinning. They too had been guilty of the same self-confidence that had spoiled his relations both with man and with God. The spiritual and moral poverty, the dissatisfaction with life that they were experiencing was, he affirmed, the result of God's determination that it should be they and not he who must give way! Yet even at their late stage in their national history, things could be put right if they began to weep, beg and cling: 'Even in the womb Jacob overreached his brother, and in manhood he strove with God. The divine angel stood firm and held his own; Jacob wept and begged favour for himself' (Hosea 12.3-4 NEB).

Luther insisted that the story of Jacob was an account of the dealing of God with his saints, so that in reading it we can continually find out what God is doing with us, and be prepared for more to come.

Thus in all the strange paradoxes that mark this incident, people in every age have been able to find parallels with what has happened to them with God, in their own lives—especially in the fact that when God is allowed to conquer man, man can himself begin to be victorious in life, in all suffering and before God.

> My will is not my own
> Till thou hast made it thine;
> If it would reach a monarch's throne
> It must its crown resign;
> It only stands unbent,
> Amid the clashing strife,
> Till on thy bosom it has leant
> And found in thee its life.
> (*George Matheson, d. 1906*)

Wilhelm Vischer quotes the passage in which Luther affirms *who* the assailant and friend of Jacob really was:

> Without the slightest contradiction this man was not an angel, but our Lord, Jesus Christ, who is the eternal God and yet was to become man whom the Jews would crucify. He was well known to the holy patriarchs, for He often appeared to them and spoke with them. Therefore He showed Himself to the fathers in such form as would indicate that He would sometime dwell with us on earth in flesh and in human form.

Vischer pleads with us to take this interpretation seriously, though at first it may appear 'fantastic'; for the central miracle of the Bible, he argues, is 'that Jesus Christ appeared as a man upon earth to wrestle with men, and to be overcome of them. In Jesus . . . the Almighty gives himself into the power of men . . . this is the message of . . . the Crucified.'

18

Postscript to Peniel

From the face of God to the face of man

The last paragraph of chapter 32 links up so closely with chapter 33 and illuminates it so much that we consider these two sections of the narrative together in our study of Jacob after Peniel.

He now goes out to meet Esau after twenty years. Esau has wandered and settled away down in the south at Seir. But he has never failed to remember his vow to kill his brother, and he has had people ready to pass on the news to him whenever Jacob made his move towards home. These facts alone explain his presence, and the four hundred armed men confirm the explanation.

Jacob, who has just *seen God face to face* (32.30), now goes out to look this man, his neighbour, Esau straight in the face. It demands courage—alone, unarmed. He has no reason to think that the rest of human life was changed when his own heart was changed. So far as he can know, the old problems outside remain the same!

Yet because he has seen the face of God, he knows that he can now face anything in the world out there, however hard, bitter, unexplainable or unjust may be what he has to meet. Nothing can really trouble him now! He has the serene consciousness that always comes to the truly forgiven sinner, that all things now will work together for good to those who love God. He goes into life, therefore, able to 'strive with men'. He has no care, for all his care is cast on God!

He takes with him to Esau the lameness that he has been dealt in his striving with God (32.31). He tries to control it,

126

and hide it, and blends it into his frequent acts of bowing (33.3). How can he explain his experience to a man like Esau—except to resort to some falsehood about tripping in the dark amongst the stones? He is strangely unafraid. There is a genuine, deep humility in his approach, but it is a humility mixed with a courage that will be put off by no difficulty. He cannot explain his feelings, but he knows in his heart, as he will express it years later, that the angel has already redeemed him 'from all evil' (cf. 48.16).

Esau

Yet something has happened even to Esau. Possibly he has enough good nature left in him to be taken aback by the sight of the defenceless wives and children (33.5-8). Possibly he has been overwhelmed by Jacob's gift! God has seen to it that the careful planning of the younger brother has not been in vain. *What do you mean by all this company which I met?* (33.8). Can this wealth be all for himself? Politely, as was the custom, he demurs from taking it. But Jacob, knowing him, wisely pleads with him to accept (33.11).

Esau is in tears. He is full of enthusiasm not only for a burial of the past but for a complete reunion. He insists that his brother enjoy his hospitality at Seir. Perhaps they could settle as family again together. Is not blood thicker than water?

Jacob has no doubt learned by experience that Esau's enthusiasms do not last long. He is cautious. He begs to be excused for refusing Esau's offer to escort him southwards—to open up and guard the way. His flocks and family cannot possibly keep up the pace that an armed posse would set. He promises to follow on slowly. He evades the generous offer of an assignment of Esau's servants to help him on his journey, for he has no intention of ever settling near Esau again.

Calvin underlines the wisdom of Jacob. His own experiences of life in the sixteenth century could show him many examples of 'proud and ferocious' men whom God had somehow miraculously restrained in a temporary way so that for a time humanity appeared in their actions even though it did not rule in their hearts. Life outside the protected zone was not all murder and rape and strife! He regards it as a miracle that Esau's mind was 'divinely moved to put on fraternal affection', but he points out that such men can 'easily be exasperated again by light causes'!

But it is more than practical wisdom which keeps Jacob detached. He believes he knows the mind of Esau. He knows that between him and his brother there are such deep differences in basic outlook on life and its problems, on God and human destiny, that in their family customs, their moral decisions, in the expression to be given to their personal aims and ambitions, there would appear such constant opposition between them that close co-operation in anything would become impossible.

Whatever judgement we ourselves may make on the situation at this point, we have to remember that the later prophets of Israel believed that the judgement of God was bound to fall on the people of Edom, the nation founded by Esau, with greater severity than elsewhere on earth (cf. Isa. 34, 63.1 ff., Jer. 49.7 ff.). It was the Edomites who gloated over the destruction of Jerusalem by the Babylonians 'Rase it, Rase it! Down to its foundations.' they cried as it was being besieged (Ps. 137.7), and they preyed on its helpless refugees (Obad. 10. ff., Ezek. 25.12 ff., 35.5).

'As into the presence of God'

It is worth pausing over the striking, though slightly enigmatic expression of feeling and self-explanation which Jacob gave in the presence of Esau before they finally parted. It is translated in the Revised Standard Version as *truly to see your face is like seeing the face of God, with such favour have you received me* (33.10).

The translation in the Jerusalem Bible, we believe, gives us a more illuminating guide to Jacob's mind: *I came into your presence as into the presence of God, but you have received me kindly.* This translation suggests to us that the night experience at Peniel brought about a profound change in Jacob's attitude to life and to other people, as well as to God. He resolves that from now on in every new emergency he meets and in each new life situation into which he enters the men and women he has now to encounter will be approached with reverence on his part. From now on his life will be lived as if he were at every moment under the grace and judgement that he has just experienced in the presence of this strong, gracious friend-adversary. He must now act and live always as one who is in fear and trembling before God, whoever be his friend or enemy. He will hold his old self captive, constrained and always in bondage while he deals with others and with the problems that face him.

He will expect nothing as his reward for it. He had expected no kindness from Esau, for he had known he deserved only judgement. The fact that Esau *had* received him kindly was from grace. He thanks God! He thanks Esau too! Even the smallest mercy that comes to him from any quarter will be noticed, and praise will be offered.

19

In the Clash of Culture

GENESIS 33.18–34.31

A piece of land

We can understand how the urge to settle down in some locality which he could legally call his 'home' came over Jacob, as it had come over Abraham and Isaac in their day. For twenty years he had been in exile, and now that he had come back to the 'promised' land he was still a pilgrim—pitching his tents either on other people's property or on common ground.

In Shechem, however, he found an extremely hospitable local people, attracted to him by his unusual wealth. They offered to sell him the plot of ground on which his tents were pitched. It was an invitation to settle. Was this approach not a sign from God that he could now begin to seek and purchase land? Possibly Jacob regarded it as a significant step towards the fulfilment of the promise when he *bought for a hundred pieces of money the piece of land on which he had pitched his tent* (33.19). To mark the significance of this gift from God he built an altar there to the *God of Israel* (33.20).

We do not wonder that the next step was fraternization with these kindly people. We are not surprised that Dinah *went out to visit the women of the land* (34.1). We can sympathize with her, since she had for so long been only one girl amongst so many boys!

The shock

Dinah was raped by Shechem the son of the local chief. It is stressed that it was a brutal act especially degrading to her womanhood. There was no attempt to obtain her consent: *He seized her, and lay with her and humbled her* (34.2).

It is important to note that amongst the local people this was not an unusual approach either to a woman or to marriage itself. There is not the least acknowledgement by Shechem that he has done anything deeply wrong. He is certain that if Dinah's family are foolish enough to feel offended, the whole matter can be put right by a handsome offer of marriage. When he decides, after having tried sex with her—for sex has the priority—that she is the kind of girl he would like to possess, he simply gives the order to his father: *Get this maiden for my wife* (34.4). Virginity either in woman or in man is of no value in his eyes.

For the sons of Jacob, however, Shechem has violated something sacred in the sight of their God. His attitude reveals to them the gulf between their family outlook and the ethos of the surrounding culture. With extraordinary speed and ferocity they determine that something must be done to restore the honour of their community in face of this sacrilege.

In this attitude we see the effect of more than three generations of the separation of their community life from the world. The experience and teaching of their fathers and mothers—Terah, Nahor, Abraham, Isaac, Rebekah, Jacob, Leah and Rachel—has gradually over the years left its deep mark on their outlook. In spite of all their faults as a family, for three generations now they have been a people living near, and under the hand of, one they know as God, wholly different in character from any of the so-called gods of other nations. Only occasionally have they found neighbours in the world around them against whom they have not required strict watchfulness. During the centuries to come the difference between their successors and the surrounding nations will become more pronounced and more clearly defined.

They not only feel contempt for the Shechemites. They feel endangered by them. The marriage that has been proposed is to be the first of many. The proposal has been coupled with an invitation to open up their family life without reserve to the natural attractions and pressures of life as it is commonly lived in the world around them: *Make marriages with us; give your daughters to us, and take our daughters for yourselves. You shall dwell with us* (34.9). If such an offer of alliance is accepted then all their standards and their mission to the world will be endangered. The invitation from the Shechemites is no less than an invitation to deny everything they owe to the God of their fathers.

An eclipse in leadership

In this crisis everything depended on whether Jacob, with all the wisdom of his years, would retain strong control over his family affairs. When the news was brought to him, his sons were in the fields, and he *held his peace until they came* (34.5). There was a family council.

It is Simeon and Levi who take over leadership, and a most discreditable and cynical plot is hatched. The offer of a total merger of families and property into one unit is accepted with the proviso that the whole tribe of Hamor be circumcised. The intention from the beginning is to murder them when their wounds have made them feverish or incapacitated.

Yet again the story stresses the danger to Israel's life should such a treaty have been taken seriously. We are made privy to the council at which Hamor and Shechem persuade their kindred to accept the condition of circumcision. It is affirmed that nothing in their old way of life will change. The wealthy and clever sons of Jacob will be absorbed, with all their property too, into the life of Shechem. The only outcome of the deal can be enormous profit for their township (34.20-4).

The fulfilment of the plot hatched by the sons of Jacob is given in revolting detail. Simeon and Levi act as bloody executioners. Younger sons come in, take the loot and deal with the women and children. God is forgotten. All decency is lost. They sink below the level of the people they are ravaging.

Jacob was obviously more shocked at the behaviour of his family than he was even over the rape of Dinah. His rebuke at the time it happened was muted—*You have brought trouble on me by making me odious* (34.30)—but his sense of shame was deep, and on his deathbed he gave expression to the disgust he felt at the incident:

Simeon and Levi are brothers;
   weapons of violence are their swords.
O my soul, come not into their council;
   O my spirit, be not joined to their
   company . . .
Cursed be their anger, for it is fierce. (49. 5ff.).

The poem shows excellent hindsight, and nobly expresses his moral indignation. Yet Jacob at that time *was* 'in their council', and his soul *was* 'joined to the company'. He failed completely to control and moderate his sons. He did not anticipate the dangers of the situation—the irreparable damage that could be done and the folly that could be worked if he abdicated leadership in such a crisis to the zealous young hotheads. Nor had he considered the danger to a child like Dinah of the policy of fraternization to which he had too easily conceded. A man of wisdom would have foreseen and tried to forestall the dangers.

'This calls for wisdom'

The writers of both Old and New Testaments often under-line the fact that along with many other gifts from God, we also need 'wisdom'. Ordinary life is so full of pitfalls and dangers that ordinary people require careful judgement and guidance from 'wise' people in order to find true fulfilment. To live in this world as the people of God with a special mission from him—as the family of Jacob had to do—has its especial dangers and requires a special kind of wisdom as well as a very great measure of ordinary common sense. It is emphasized in the New Testament that, as the centuries pass, as the end of history approaches, as human affairs become more complicated, and human evil more daemonic and desperate, there will be more and more need for the gift of such wisdom by the people of God (cf. Rev. 13.18).

We are frequently urged by the biblical writers to cultivate such a gift (Prov. 4.5, James 1.5). If we could define with precision its various aspects, we would certainly include the ability to judge accurately our present situation with all its possibilities and dangers, to read the future from the present and to see clearly the consequences of our actions, especially those which might arise from foolish, hasty or ignorant decisions.

The measure of ordinary wisdom which a person possesses is often dependent on experience of life—but if it is lacking it can be cultivated, and we have been given the books of Proverbs and Ecclesiastes and Job in the Bible in order to help us to attain it through reading and study. But above all, we are told, the Spirit of God is able to help us to acquire a divine wisdom directly from God himself.

We need not be too surprised that Jacob, who was chosen by God to be such a good pioneer for us in matters like personal devotion to God, the way of prayer and the meaning of human destiny, was not at the same time a model of wisdom. God does not endow one man with all the gifts the

Church requires for his service. Moreover, the community wisdom, which was later to be such an important feature of the life of Israel, took many years to accumulate and to become a shared possession among the people of God. We shall see that, in the generation after Jacob, his son Joseph will become the model of a wise, statesman-like man of God, expert in foresight. After Joseph, people like David and Solomon will take the lead in an age in which wisdom is cultivated.

We are fortunate to have this story in Genesis 34, at least to show us how much we need such wisdom and how tragic the consequences can become when older people, who may be expected to possess it, neglect their responsibility for leadership and allow the enthusiasm of the immature and the folly of the obstinate to take control without check or restraint. Great damage is often done in personal, social and church life, because people are not given warnings by those who should know better.

One never-changing issue

Though Simeon and Levi are condemned for their anger and infamous acts of violence, they are not condemned for their indignation over the rape of their sister, or for their zeal in seeking to maintain the 'difference' between themselves and the surrounding peoples which they felt to be so important—especially in such a matter as the approach to marriage. Indeed, the story is told in such a way that we are led to sense an ultimate good in what they were trying to achieve, and the tragedy is intensified for us simply because the intention was good.

The reason for their outrage is clearly brought out. They felt that their sister had been *defiled* (34.5, 27) and their family life had been defiled. Their standard is clearly defined. *Such a thing* as sexual intercourse before marriage *ought not to be done* (34.7). Even for a woman to offer her

135

body in such a way would have been to act *like a harlot*, and for a man to take her was to make her such (34.31).

In holding such views Simeon and Levi are in line with the central clear and uncompromising thrust of the teaching of the whole Bible on such a matter. As we read through the Bible we find that it in no way relaxes in its extraordinarily high expectation of premarital chastity amongst the people of God, and of faithfulness to the vows implied in the marriage bond.

The more fully the people of God come to understand him and his will for human life, the more clearly they come to realize that such knowledge and privilege as they enjoy binds them to live quite different lives in quite a different kind of society from those around who have no such understanding of true worship, true justice and love. In this development it becomes more and more clear that one aspect of their way of life that distinguishes them from all other nations is their attitude and conduct in matters of sex and marriage.

This is clearly brought out, for instance, in the long and dramatic story of David's later life. One step backwards into pagan indulgence by King David is seen to plunge him into a fatal course of deceit and murder. And after it has happened he and his family are involved in the most bitter sorrow. In the midst of the series of tragedies that follow so surely on his sin, the same plea as we heard from Simeon and Levi we now hear from Tamar (2 Sam. 13).

When Amnon, Tamar's own half-brother, attempts to rape her, she appeals to him at least to obtain the king's permission and to marry her before he takes his pleasure, for she pleads, 'such a thing is not done in Israel'. Of course it was done everywhere else in the world. It was approved of, too, by worldly, progressive members of the Israelite community like Jonadab, Amnon's elderly psychological counsellor. But Tamar, a true witness to Israel's best conscience and Israel's God, knew as Simeon and Levi had known that it could not be done in a nation that knew and loved God in truth.

We do not find that this outlook alters in any way in the New Testament, with its repeated appeals to Christians in the midst of the Roman world to make the difference between them and their pagan neighbours manifestly clear at this very point (Acts 15.20; Thess. 4.3), and its repeated affirmation that by the power of the risen Christ such a way is now possible to follow (e.g. 1 Cor. 6.9-11). Such an attitude is of course far from our current outlook today.

We can best understand some of the Old Testament stories when we study them in the light of their movement towards Christ. The climax of Israel's history occurred when the Word of God came to the virgin Mary: 'Hail O favoured one, the Lord is with you', and she replied, 'Behold I am the handmaid of the Lord' (Luke 2.28, 38). The woman, in Israel, is therefore of prime importance. At this crucial moment she is to be the sole representative of the people of God—and her male partner is left standing on the side-lines. Israel is to find its true meaning in producing this virgin, Mary, and in presenting her to God.

The difference in the approach to sex and marriage between Israel and other nations had its roots in such a purpose of God. Of course Simeon, Levi and the sons of Jacob had no notion that this was why they felt their difference so important to maintain. But are we not justified, looking back, in seeing this as an unconscious reason why they rejected Shechem so violently. Mary could never have been produced by a nation that did not foster her type. It is because of her that premarital chastity was of prime importance for Israel's womanhood. And because of this it was of primary importance for Israel's manhood too.

20

Back to Bethel

GENESIS 35.1—36.43

Heart searching

The events which took place at Shechem made clear to Jacob what had been clear to Abraham—that the possession of the land by the people of God would be brought about in God's own way in God's own time, and it would come to Israel as God's gift. Moreover the unity and peace that must finally be sought between Israel and the surrounding nations would never be brought about by ignoring the differences between them. With each generation such differences were becoming more complicated and deeper. The threat Jacob felt to the safety of his family forced him to make preparations for flight from the plot of land on the possession of which he had come to place too much significance.

It was no surprise, therefore, when the call came from God: *Arise, go up to Bethel, and dwell there; and make there an altar to the God who appeared to you when you fled from your brother Esau* (35.1).

He blamed himself for what had happened. He blamed his family too. He had been too weak, they had been too cruel! He knew that behind all their failures there had been one common cause. They had all to some extent lost touch with the living God, and thus they had lost sight of some aspects of his truth and his mercy. This loss must be restored. Jacob remembered how his flight from Esau had led him at Bethel into a great new beginning in his early life. Might not his flight from Shechem with his whole family, led by the same grace, into the same place, also become a

138

means of entering with them all into a closer walk with God in the future?

As he took his way he received a sign of encouragement: *As they journeyed, a terror from God fell upon the cities that were round about them, so that they did not pursue the sons of Jacob* (35.5). Later, his successors were to find themselves often saved by God in battle, in exactly the same way. As a nation they would never be able to develop and muster on their side the skills and the resources to enable them to survive in a world that was to become alienated from them because of their independence and exclusiveness, but God would control the hearts and minds of their enemies, and among those whom he did not incline to favour his people, he would spread unreasonable fears, so that they were often made free when they could have been destroyed.

Repentance towards forgiveness

Jacob arranges that, even though a flight, the journey will become also a solemn religious pilgrimage, an act of worship, a work of repentance expressing their contrition as they seek again the assurance of God's forgiveness. Jacob calls his family to such repentance: *Put away the foreign gods that are among you, and purify yourselves, and change your garments; then let us arise and go up to Bethel* (35.2-3). They must undertake the journey in an attitude and state of holiness. Von Rad at this point in his commentary helpfully defines this holiness for us: 'Holiness in the Old Testament is the state of belonging to God. Therefore it requires a kind of confessional renunciation of everything unholy, and a cultic symbolic declaration of his (the worshipper's) desire for purification and for clarification of his relation to God.' It is to be a journey of repentance, moving towards the realization of an already promised forgiveness.

We must not affirm that the forgiveness and renewal which they expected to receive at Bethel was dependent on the degree of repentance and holiness they achieved as they made the journey. After all, Jacob's previous experience of God's forgiving grace at Bethel had brought him full forgiveness even though he had shown few previous signs of repentance. His repentance on that occasion had seemed to follow his forgiveness. Yet here God seems to some extent to reverse this order. Though he pledges his forgiveness he seems to desire some sign of repentance on their way to receive it. We have exactly the same order in Isaiah's early preaching to Judah. They are first called on to make themselves clean and to put away their evil, and after this command is given comes the invitation to enter the experience of forgiveness (cf. Isa. 1.16-18). With God we find that repentance and forgiveness are very closely bound up together. We cannot have one without the other. And, as happens clearly in the New Testament too, sometimes one is offered and asked for first, sometimes the other (cf. Acts 2.38, 5.31, Mark 2.5).

Postscripts

The rest of the 35th chapter (and the 36th too) reads like a series of postscripts to the section of the book of Genesis which we have been studying. It precedes the beginning of a very distinct new story, which, we find, also continues the story of Jacob.

We read of the death of Rebekah's nurse Deborah (35.8). This mention raises many questions to which no answer is indicated. How did she come to be in the company? Did Rebekah send her on after Jacob, back to Paddan-aram to be a help to him during the early years before he had Leah or Rachel? Or did she travel home herself after Rebekah died? In any case she was an influential link with the piety of the line of Abraham and the line of Nahor. Jacob's family therefore grew up in Paddan-aram, not simply with Jacob as the sole witness to the teaching of Abraham, but with this godly woman alongside them.

Moreover, Deborah is one of the great multitude of ordinary people in the Bible whom we discover only occasionally when they are suddenly mentioned as playing a small part in what is going on, yet who nevertheless create the conditions in which the work of the greater heroes and heroines of the faith can be successful.

We read of the birth of Benjamin and the death of Rachel. In her weakness, pain and sorrow she gives him the name Benoni ('son of my sorrow'). In days when the giving of a name was regarded as prophetic of a child's destiny, to be called such a sad name might have put a mark on the child's temperament. Jacob, though grief-stricken himself, took the responsibility of cancelling this shadow and insisted on the name 'Benjamin' ('son of my right hand—35.16-21).

We read of what must have caused Jacob yet another type of grief; *Reuben went and lay with Bilhah his father's concubine; and Israel heard of it* (35.22). Israel *eventually* heard about it: the implication is that many of his sons' doings never reached Jacob's ears. On hearing of this misdeed he was so stunned and numbed that he failed at the time to express his sorrow. Calvin suggests that the narrator himself chooses to pass over all comment on what this meant at the time to Jacob because he found his own rhetoric inadequate:

> Moses only relates that Jacob was informed of this crime; but he conceals his grief, not because he was unfeeling . . . but because his grief was too great to be expressed. For here Moses seems to have acted as the painter did who, in representing the sacrifice of Iphigena, put a veil over her father's face, because he could not sufficiently express the grief of his countenance.

If Reuben's name is so obviously mentioned as if first in

honour in the following list of the twelve sons of Jacob, it is 'that he may be loaded with greater opprobrium'.

Finally, Isaac *breathed his last; old and full of days*. He had lived to see Jacob's family growing and prospering and his two sons reconciled. *Esau and Jacob buried him* (35.29).

Acknowledgements

Unless otherwise indicated, the Scripture quotations in this publication are from the Revised Standard Version of the Bible, copyrighted 1946 and 1952 by the Division of Christian Education of the National Council of the Churches of Christ in the USA.

Extracts from the New English Bible, second edition © 1970, are used by permission of Oxford and Cambridge University Presses.

The quotations from Calvin's *Commentary on Genesis* are from the Calvin Society edition, Edinburgh, 1847.

The quotations from Luther are from his *Lectures on Genesis* (Luther's Works, Vols. 5-6), Concordia Publishing House, St Louis, 1960-4.

Works consulted and referred to are:

Cassuto, U., *A Commentary on the Book of Genesis*. The Hebrew University, Jerusalem, 1961.

Jacob, B., *The First Book of the Bible, Genesis*. KTAV Publishers, New York, 1974.

Kidner, D., *Genesis* (Tyndale Commentaries). Inter-Varsity Press, London, 1967.

Mays, J. L., *Hosea* (Old Testament Library). SCM Press, London, 1972.

ACKNOWLEDGEMENTS

Sarna, N. B., *Understanding Genesis*. Jewish Theological Seminary of America, New York, 1966.

Vischer, W., *The Witness of the Old Testament to Christ* (English translation). Lutterworth Press, London, 1949.

von Rad, G., *Genesis* (Old Testament Library). SCM Press, London, 1972.

Weiser, A., *The Psalms* (Old Testament Library). SCM Press, London, 1962.